I0214516

The Golden Age of Indianapolis Theaters

The

GOLDEN
AGE *of*

Indianapolis
Theaters

HOWARD CALDWELL

QUARRY BOOKS

AN IMPRINT OF
INDIANA UNIVERSITY PRESS
BLOOMINGTON AND INDIANAPOLIS

This book is a publication of

Quarry Books
an imprint of

Indiana University Press
601 North Morton Street
Bloomington, Indiana 47404-3797 USA

www.iupress.indiana.edu

Telephone orders   800-842-6796
Fax orders   812-855-7931
Orders by e-mail   iuporder@indiana.edu

© 2010 by Howard Caldwell
All rights reserved

No part of this book may be reproduced
or utilized in any form or by any means,
electronic or mechanical, including
photocopying and recording, or by any
information storage and retrieval system,
without permission in writing from the
publisher. The Association of American
University Presses' Resolution on Permis-
sions constitutes the only exception to
this prohibition.

⊖ The paper used in this publication meets
the minimum requirements of the Ameri-
can National Standard for Information
Sciences—Permanence of Paper for
Printed Library Materials,
ANSI Z39.48-1992.

Manufactured in the United
States of America

Library of Congress Cataloging-in-
Publication Data

Caldwell, Howard, [date]
  The golden age of Indianapolis theaters /
Howard Caldwell.
      p. cm.
  Includes bibliographical references.
  ISBN 978-0-253-35460-0 (cl : alk. paper)
  1. Theaters—Indiana—Indianapolis—
History. 2. Motion picture theaters—
Indiana—Indianapolis—History. I. Title.
  PN2277.I5C35 2010
  792.09772′52—dc22

                              2009051721

  1 2 3 4 5 15 14 13 12 11 10

To Martha Freeman Caldwell
my grandmother,
who introduced me to
the theater world

CONTENTS

PREFACE

I've decided that the desire to write this book is connected with what was going on in the theater world at the time of my birth. Movies were beginning to talk, and theaters soon began booking swing music orchestras that were becoming headliners themselves.

In our homes, quite often we were introduced to entertainers on radio, which fired us up to see them in a film or on the stage. As for the orchestras, we heard them on radio and on our 78 rpm record players before we saw them in person.

Theaters were elegantly built and offered us entertainment in the daytime and in the evening. Prices were within our budgets if we managed to have a paper route or worked in a drugstore or helped a neighbor with yard work. Dating usually began at the neighborhood theaters (where some of us were hired as ushers). But for me it was the downtown first-run palaces that were awesome.

Maturity begins to add obligations that may weaken our less significant pleasures, but for my generation World War II didn't chase movies and onstage entertainers away. They continued to be a part of our lives on military bases and for me on a ship. They made an important contribution to morale.

Back home again, my interest continued but in a different way as television moved in and the theaters we once knew faded away or were converted to other uses.

All the early days of theater entertainment became happy memories. Those memories were subjects that interested not only my generation but some of the others, too. I began delivering talks about it all. Audiences began sharing their memories and were asking about locations and names of various theaters.

The city lost a theater specialist early in 2009. Fredrick Vollrath lived to be eighty-six after converting his home to a private museum, bursting with theater and movie memorabilia. When Loew's closed in 1970, Vollrath acquired the box office along with light fixtures, an urn, lion heads, signs, and post displays. He had a theater downstairs with a projection booth allowing him to show features from his large collection (4,000 on discs), most of them classic novels, musicals, and comedies spanning fifty years.

Vollrath was the ultimate example of a passion that triggered his decision to retire at the age of fifty-eight. He served Indiana Bell for over forty years. It was one of the many reasons I decided to bring back those memories for others who might find them as fascinating as they have been for me. While Vollrath collected memorabilia, his brain was filled with theater knowledge. Call out the name of a theater, and he would tell you where it was, when it opened, and its contribution to theater history.

This book was written with personal references that I hoped would make it a little clearer to those out of my age bracket. I think it needs to be told. It starts with little support from the city's population. Slowly it begins to be accepted and fans begin to appear. Movies won them over quickly, and sound sent them to higher levels. Gradually they lost their dominance but never disappeared. They survived in spite of heavy competition.

ACKNOWLEDGMENTS

I have a number of people to thank for helping me in the process of assembling this theater story. One of the first is Corbin Patrick, whom I used to encounter between newscasts taking his dinner break before arriving at a theater for one of his many reviews. He encouraged me to move ahead and made himself available. Author-photographer-jazz music specialist Duncan Schiedt was another one I could turn to for help on research and photographs.

As a longtime member of the Indiana Historical Society, I turned to staff members frequently, and they were most helpful. The same thing happened when I communicated with *Indianapolis Star* editor Dennis Ryerson, who turned me over to archive specialist Dawn Mitchell and photographer Joe Young to find photos of people and theaters.

A'Lelia Bundles, author-journalist and the great-great-granddaughter of Madame C. J. Walker, provided insight in describing "the first self-made American millionaire through hair care products sales and real estate investments." Ms. Bundles graciously provided a photo of Madame Walker, who saw to it that when she moved her company headquarters to Indianapolis, black citizens also would soon have an elegant theater that would welcome them.

Highly regarded jazz musician Reginald Du Valle (now deceased) provided an onstage picture of his father and his musicians, who appeared on the Walker Theater stage when it opened.

Other musicians who helped were orchestra leader Kay Kyser and Virginia Byrd, younger sister of Dessa. Assistance came from two researchers, Fredrick Vollrath and Charles Eiler. Anecdotes came from two theater employees, Nick Longworth at the Sanders and the Granada and a teenage usher at the Circle, Carl Stotts.

Almarie Huffman Burke, the late Vincent Burke's daughter-in-law, helped me learn about the longtime manager of English's Theater. Mrs. Richard Beck (Rosemary) was helpful because her father, Oskar Edmond Browne, served as musical director at English's when she was growing up.

Another type of help came from family members. Wife Lynn's patience with the chaos in my den during the last many, many months was eloquent. With daughter Susan Hutchins leading the way, the trip through the acquisition of a new computer and its puzzlement for a senior citizen author also was eloquent. Other members of this family team were two grandsons, Sean and Michael Reidy, and their father, Dan.

Some IU Press folks helped out, too!

The Golden Age of
Indianapolis Theaters

1

Birth of a Theater Buff

In 1934, downtown theater offerings opened on Friday at 11 AM and ran through Thursday. Children's tickets cost a dime, and adults (12 and older) paid a quarter. Ticket prices rose slightly after 6 PM. Courtesy *Indianapolis News*.

I t all started on one of those partly cloudy, chilly January mornings in Indianapolis. The sun was making an effort to better the situation with little success. But to an eight-year-old boy, it was an inspirational day, free of rules imposed by a teacher in an elementary classroom. It was a Saturday in 1934.

As I arose from bed to meet the youthful challenges of the day, I heard Grandmother Caldwell rustling about, preparing for a trip downtown. She loved to shop at her favorite stores, L. S. Ayres and the William H. Block Co., although she rarely made any purchases. She had spent earlier years selling women's hats, and I always suspected that even more than shopping she enjoyed visiting with store clerks, comparing careers.

Seated at what I considered an ancient wooden two-leaf table where breakfast was served at my home, Grandmother suddenly turned to Mother and said, "Maybe Howard would like to accompany me on this trip." I was only mildly interested until she uttered the magic words: "Maybe he and I could find a show we'd like to see."

I knew it was going to happen when Mother didn't protest. I immediately found the morning newspaper and that special page with the theater advertisements. The one that jumped out at me was the Loew's Palace ad declaring that "the high-hatted tragedian of song, Ted Lewis and his Musical Klowns," were appearing onstage. That was my choice.

Grandmother wasn't so sure about my preference. She was leaning toward an all-film program at the Indiana. It was *Easy to Love* with Mary Astor, Adolphe Menjou, and Edward Everett Horton. I persisted, and she surrendered eventually. I had an advantage. I was her only grandson.

Our home on Bosart Avenue was only a half block north of East Washington Street, where streetcars were passing by every few minutes. For a fare of 7¢ we could travel downtown in a matter of fifteen minutes. I tolerated the shopping part of the trip by clinging to Grandmother's promise that we would head to the theater (first block on North Pennsylvania Street) by 10:45 AM when the theater box office opened. She was true to her word.

We located ourselves in the lower balcony. We admired the plain yet severe-looking curtain that concealed the stage. It had the word *Asbestos* in large letters across its middle. Grandmother explained its importance. It was fireproof and would protect us if flames suddenly broke out backstage. That had happened to theaters in earlier years, before electricity was used and when lighting was primitive.

This pre-show time also included orchestral music that Grandmother called canned music. She explained that it had been recorded and that only a few years previously such music would have been provided by an orchestra in the Loew's pit. Suddenly the asbestos curtain disappeared, revealing a glittery blue curtain that would eventually part and reveal a movie screen. The lights lowered, and the film program began.

The Loew's feature was *Sons of the Desert* with comics Stan Laurel and Oliver Hardy. I thought it was hilarious. The uncomplicated plot involves two neighbors who convince their wives with the help of a phony doctor that one of them is ill and needs a week in Hawaii. The "doctor," of course, advises that it would be best if both made the trip.

Once free to travel, the husbands (Laurel and Hardy) head to Chicago for a convention of their lodge (Sons of the Desert) previously vetoed by the wives. The naïve spouses learn the truth when they attend a neighborhood movie theater and see their husbands waving and smiling in a convention parade during a newsreel. The rest of the feature deals with the unsuspecting pair's unexpected homecoming provided by their angry wives.

3

My grandmother, Martha Caldwell, was our family's movie fan and critic. Photographer unknown.

Following some short subjects (news and previews of the next week's show), the spotlight shifted to the stage and bandleader-host Ted Lewis. He tantalized us by doing his first vocal number in front of the glittery curtain with his musicians playing out of sight behind him. Ted was singing about his old top hat (one of his trademarks). Grandmother loved it and leaned over to tell me she was pleased with our choice after all.

The curtain parted, introducing us to the orchestra as Lewis moved about the stage gracefully, doing another number, a favorite of his, "When My Baby Smiles at Me." From time to time he would call out, "Is everybody happy?" It assured him of shouts of glee and applause from the audience. Just why he called his musicians "Klowns" escapes me, but I suspect he wasn't quite sure yet that a band alone was a safe audience draw. That would come later when the big band era would produce stars based on their musical talents and popularity. Each Lewis band number included little personal touches by Ted (a frown, a smile, or comic body language) to guarantee audience attention.

Grandmother and I were dazzled by it all, and we weren't alone. *Indianapolis Star* reviewer Richard Tucker called the show "almost too good to be true in timing and sophistication."

With one alteration, the Saturday trips downtown continued. No longer would I accompany my grandmother during the shopping part of the journey. She would get me to the first show, do her shopping, and then join me for the second round. I saw everything twice.

Although Loew's Palace was one of our regular Saturday haunts, it would rarely involve a movie accompanied by a stage show again. One exception was a week when Cab Calloway and his Cotton Club Revue orchestra appeared. The mid-1930s, however, found most of the big downtown theaters turning exclusively to movie programs. For example, the Palace, as it later was known, introduced Indianapolis and the surrounding area to the very popular Metro-Goldwyn-Mayer productions.

Some of our special delights included the Thin Man series, starring William Powell and Myrna Loy, Wallace Beery and Jackie Cooper in *Treasure Island,*

Freddie Bartholomew in *David Copperfield,* Jeanette MacDonald and Nelson Eddy in *Naughty Marietta,* and the unforgettable Andy Hardy series with Mickey Rooney.

Looking back now, I suspect Mother and Grandmother had an approved list for which theaters we patronized. Besides Loew's, there were the Apollo, Indiana, and Circle. The Apollo was where we saw all the Shirley Temple adventures and the popular Will Rogers films. When the humorist-philosopher died in a plane crash in 1935, many of his films were shown again at the Apollo, drawing capacity audiences, Grandmother and myself included.

The mighty Indiana, the largest theater in the state, also was running mostly films in the mid-1930s, although it had a sophisticated stage at its disposal. This is where Grandmother and I saw the early Bing Crosby and Bob Hope films (before they teamed up for the Road series) and the Fred Astaire and Ginger Rogers epics. The Circle and Indiana took turns on which theater got what first, since both were owned by the same local corporation, known as the Circle Theater, Inc.

By this time, I had recovered from seeing my first talking picture. I remember burying my head in a jacket when three males with loud voices appeared on the screen. I was convinced they would jump out at me any moment. Photographer unknown.

During the mid-1930s, our grandmother-grandson team never went near the Lyric, even though it had stage shows most weeks. I only guess now that some of the vaudeville acts and revues featuring scantily clad females (shown in newspaper advertisements) weren't considered advisable entertainment for children. The Colonial (later the Fox), of course, was way out of bounds. It was the city's longtime burlesque house, located on North Illinois Street just across from the YMCA (more about all these theaters later).

Another theater I never considered visiting was the Capitol at 148 W. Washington Street. It became a burlesk (its spelling) house in its declining years. By the 1930s it would become a second-run, low-price movie house. During its long history it had several names, but old-timers would remember it as the Park. Historians knew it as the city's first theater structure when it opened as the Metropolitan.

5

Theater One and
What Happened Before

I t was opening night. Not just any opening night. This was the moment when Indianapolis's first theater, the Metropolitan, would open its doors to an audience. The date was September 27, 1858.

This was no small enterprise. The orchestra seating (also known as a theater's first floor) could accommodate 827 customers, the balcony another 900. The *Indianapolis Morning Journal* offered these words after touring the premises:

> No expense has been spared to render the Metropolitan the most elegant theater in the west. The auditorium, proscenium, and private boxes have been furnished in the most elaborate style of art. . . . The ventilation and view from all parts of the house is believed to be perfect.

The most expensive seats were the private boxes ($5), but all the others ranged from 25¢ to 50¢. Just how many of these seats were occupied that first night was not mentioned in stories that appeared in both the *Journal* and the *Indianapolis Daily Sentinel.*

At 7:30 PM the stage curtain was raised, and the theater's musicians played "The Star-Spangled Banner." E. T. Sherlock, the manager, who had leased the facility, introduced the actors and actresses, all members of the new theater's stock company. They were a sizable group of twenty-three with their leading member, H. M. Gossin, identified in advertisements as a "talented young tragedian."

That September evening the company presented a drama titled *Love's Sacrifice,* along with what was promoted as a "laughable farce," *My Neighbor's Wife.* The following evening the company was joined by the Keller troupe of sixty, who were

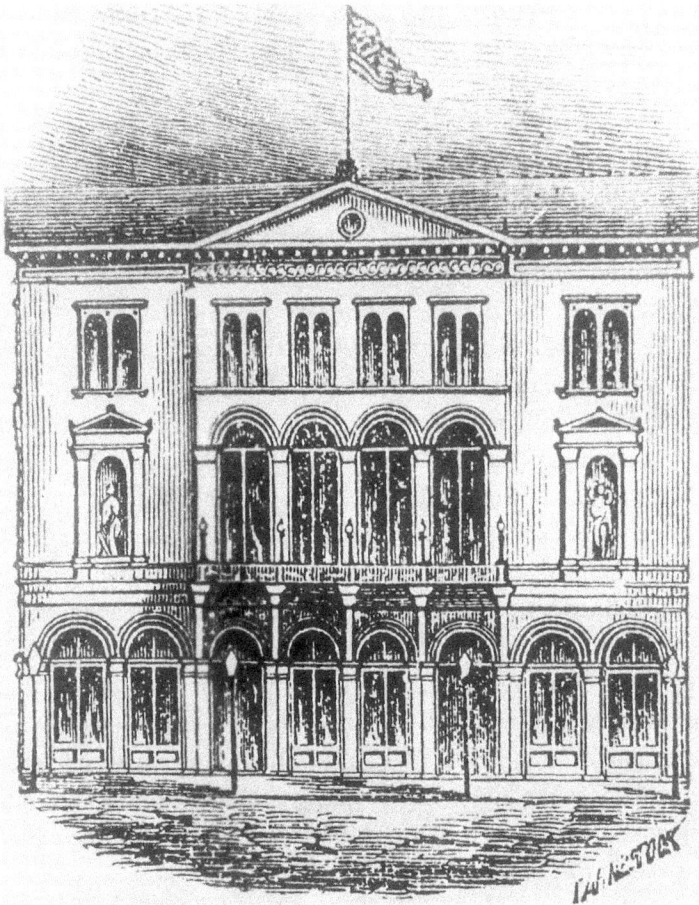

Local businessman Valentine Butsch purchased the site and built the Metropolitan for $60,000. Typical of the era, the theater (or hall, as it was sometimes called) had a stage and seats on an upper floor. The ground floor was leased to retail outlets. Photographer unknown.

known as "living picture artists." Picturesque tableaux offered by such groups were quite popular in the early years of theater. They also sometimes provided scenes that bred controversy.

Tuesday morning, just hours before the Keller troupe was to appear on the Metropolitan's brand-new stage, an item criticizing its recent performance in Cincinnati appeared in the "Letters to the Editor" section of the *Journal*. A reader had provided the newspaper with a theater review by the *Cincinnati Gazette* of a performance there the previous Saturday night. The reviewer had denounced the troupe for attempting a representation of God in one of its tableaux, which it described as "impious and blasphemous."

The Keller troupe appeared Tuesday anyway, but did not present the tableau in question. Actually, the controversy provided the theater with some added publicity. More customers showed up on Tuesday than were there for the opening. The following morning, the *Journal* contained more information from the Cincin-

9

nati newspaper, but this time it was backing down and had accepted the troupe's argument that it was depicting Adam, not God. The troupe came out ahead, and so did the new theater.

During the next few weeks, the stock company offered audiences an array of dramas and farces, changing selections almost nightly. In October, newspaper advertisements promoted a weeklong appearance of Miss Sallie St. Clair, a well-known actress of the time. She played leading roles in a different play each night. Performances were offered Monday through Saturday. A city ordinance prevented any shows on Sunday.

There was one other little blip in the early weeks of the theater's offerings. On October 25, J. H. Hackett came to the theater for a two-day engagement. His impact was not what the Metropolitan expected. He was promoted as a "celebrated comedian, engaged at great expense." He appeared as Falstaff in *Henry IV*. The trouble came over a farce he also starred in that night that shocked the *Journal*. The paper called it "immoral, obscene, disgusting." The article also took aim at Sherlock: "A theater will always exist in Indianapolis. It has languished because the gross, and not the refined taste, was catered to by our dramatic managers."

In his two-volume history, *Greater Indianapolis,* Jacob Piatt Dunn reminds us that there were strong elements of morality in the new growing city at this time. For example, in the early nineteenth century, dancing was not tolerated by Methodists, Presbyterians, or Baptists. Writes Dunn, "If nothing worse, it [dancing] was frivolous and consequently young people of religious families did not dance or go to dancing parties." One might add that, since the theater frequently featured dancers, it was not a popular attraction for many citizens.

There were other moral issues. Performers in the theater were looked down upon by many as unstable and unreliable. At the time the Metropolitan opened, W. R. Holloway made this observation in his 1870 book, *Indianapolis: A Historical and Statistical Sketch of the Railroad City:*

> Although Indianapolis holds a high place in the estimation of showmen and is
> invariably marked for every traveling exhibition, from an operatic star to a double-
> headed baby, a considerable portion of its respectable patronage has been directed
> by a peculiarity of taste, compounded by Puritan traditions and partly of backwoods
> culture, which even to this day, makes certain classes of entertainments unclean.

Ironically, after a brief cooling-off period, the once critical *Journal* did a turn-around and began bragging about the stage efforts at the Metropolitan. In December, when the theater provided a professional production of *Uncle Tom's Cabin,* the *Journal* described Mary McVicker's portrayal of Eva as the best in the country.

In January 1859, the Metropolitan introduced opera to Indianapolis. Cooper's English Opera troupe presented a different production each night during a four-day visit. The *Journal* was ecstatic and even editorialized about this historic event, crediting Sherlock with "endeavoring to cater to refined and cultivated tastes."

Unfortunately for Sherlock, a more favorable press did not mean all was well. His efforts were not producing enough dollars. There also was evidence that citizen hostility continued to be a problem. When the theater's manager offered to present a benefit for the local widows and orphans' society, it was refused on moral grounds, convincing owner Valentine Butsch that some changes were needed. He replaced Sherlock and dismissed the stock company, a move that provided more flexibility in booking attractions. Butsch also made the building available to political conventions and other organizations. He even dropped the word *theater* from his facility's title and renamed it Metropolitan Hall.

Butsch's decision to stay with his theater still made sense. Ever since the state legislature created Indianapolis in 1821 by deciding it should be the state's capital (it officially became that in 1825), it had experienced rapid growth. It grew from two or three families in 1820 to more than 18,000 by the time the Metropolitan opened. The population increased considerably during the next twenty years to 70,000 in 1880.

Darrell Gooch (my speech and theater instructor at Howe High School in the early 1940s) did his master of arts thesis on the nineteenth-century theater era of Indianapolis. He noted the significance of two developments taking place early in the century: the appearance of National Road and railroad tracks. In 1830, the road reached Indianapolis from the east from as far away as Baltimore. Later it would extend west to St. Louis. It was not easy traveling at first. Many tree stumps and poor drainage contributed to that, but eventually it got better. An even more significant creation for traveling performers was train travel.

• • • • • • • • • • • • •

Uncle Tom's Cabin was originally a successful book written by Harriet Beecher Stowe. It was published just six years before the Metropolitan opened, with its critical look at the slavery states in the United States. It became highly popular in the North onstage, and traveling companies presented it numerous times in Indianapolis. The author's brother had an Indianapolis connection. Henry Ward Beecher was the first pastor at Second Presbyterian Church. He served from 1839 until 1847. He left to become pastor of the Plymouth Presbyterian Church in Boston.

• • • • • • • • • • • • •

11

Railroad service in and out of Indianapolis was born in 1847 with the completion of tracks from Madison, Indiana. Gooch noted that by 1880, "twelve radiating railroads were constructed connecting the city with Chicago, Cleveland, St. Louis, Louisville, Columbus, and New York." His point, of course, was that it greatly enhanced the opportunity to book traveling actors and production crews.

In his book *Indianapolis Union Station,* James Hetherington notes that the railroad benefit for Indianapolis occurred quickly, after 1860, providing an additional plus for the new theater: travel opportunities for out-of-town customers:

> Five railroad trunk lines crossed the state, running east and west. Three other systems went the length of the state, north and south. With about forty more small railroads in service by this time, most of Indiana's cities and towns were served by rail. Indianapolis had become the center of this rail network.

Although the Metropolitan was the city's first theater structure, it was not the first to introduce the city's citizens to theater entertainment. Traveling performers previously had been booked at a variety of structures that were altered for that use.

The initial effort on New Year's Eve of 1824 was a disaster. It took place at Carter's Tavern, identified as a double log cabin, east of Illinois and north of Washington Street. A Mr. and Mrs. Smith convinced the owner, Mr. Carter, that their show would be refined and genteel. The dining room was filled to capacity when the curtain rose, revealing an improvised stage, lighted by coal oil lamps. As described in Edward Leary's book, *Indianapolis: The Story of a City,* the opening number was provided by Mrs. Smith, wearing a sweeping skirt of velvet and satin, who sang "The Star-Spangled Banner." This was followed immediately by fiddler Billy Bagwell's rendition of a fast jig-time tune. At this point, Mrs. Smith, now blindfolded, went into her specialty, a sailor's hornpipe in and around several dozen eggs, which she promised she would not break. Owner Carter, an elder of the Baptist church, afraid that such music would offend his customers, ordered the performance stopped and demanded that the performers confine their music to hymns and psalms.

After a hurried conference, the show resumed with a musical skit that was not compatible with the music Carter had demanded. The audience responded with laughter and jeers. The curtain was lowered, ending the city's first attempt at offering some of its citizens a look at show biz.

3

A War's Effect and
Another Theater Is Born

T he Metropolitan had a busy if not especially profitable third season (1860–61). Valentine Butsch brought in a stock company that featured a "celebrated comedienne and vocalist," Marian McCarthy, and a "well known comedian," Felix Vincent. The company listed eighteen performers.

Home-based stock companies were used by many American theaters during the nineteenth century. This reduced the uncertainties of travel, which still had its problems, and the system was less costly. However, prior to the Civil War, it did not guarantee success in Indianapolis.

Evidence that the Metropolitan's company was not breaking any financial records was apparent when the season suddenly ended early in March 1861. Six weeks later, the country was in a war. Patriotism reached a new level, and it was felt that a theater could provide an outlet for expressing it. The company was recalled for a theater reopening April 25, and it remained there well into the month of August. Just days after the Confederate attack on Fort Sumter, a patriotic concert was held at the theater featuring Mme. Ines Fabbri, who sang "The Star-Spangled Banner" in the costume of the Goddess of Liberty. It prompted glowing reviews from the local press.

By the time the theater reopened, the state legislature was meeting in a special session and the city was filled with soldiers and what Jacob Piatt Dunn called "enthusiastic townsmen." Many of them crowded into the Metropolitan, where patriotic emotions were at fever pitch night after night. Notes Dunn: "After that spring there was never any hostile criticism of the theater, as an institution, in the Indianapolis newspapers."

On January 1, 1862, the Met, as it frequently was called, launched the new year with what it promoted as the "great drama" of *The Southern Rebellion,* starring Vincent and McCarthy. The theater advertisements said it would appear at the theater until further notice. It lasted just four days. However, the theater remained busy with other bookings.

The first nationally recognized actor to play the Met was John Wilkes Booth. He opened a six-day engagement on Christmas Day, 1861. He was highly regarded at the time, appearing in six leading roles in a Shakespearian lineup that included *Macbeth, Hamlet,* and *Richard III.* He was referred to in those days as the "celebrated tragedian" and the "great Booth." He returned for one week in November 1862 and five weeks later in January 1863. The last visit came fifteen months before he would assassinate Abraham Lincoln at the Ford Theater.

For six years (1862–68) the Metropolitan offered the growing city of Indianapolis some of the best theater talent available. Frequently the productions were selections from Shakespeare. Besides Booth, there were appearances by John Neafie, Daniel Bandmann, and Lawrence Barrett. Women, who were limited when it came to professional careers, were finding success in the new world of American theater. Emma Waller, Miss Lotta, Fanny Price, and Emily Melville all had leading roles at the Metropolitan, but they have left little imprint all these years later.

A key booking during this first decade at the Metropolitan was a musical-melodrama titled *Black Crook,* which *The Oxford Companion to American Theatre* describes as "the most successful Broadway play up to its time and the first to run for over a year." The production had opened in New York City in September 1866 and was on the road appearing in Indianapolis a year later. Metropolitan advertisements declared that it would appear "every evening until further notice." The engagement ran for an unprecedented fifteen days.

What was the appeal of this show, which would net over $1 million? It had a fairyland theme and what Daniel Blum's *Pictorial History of American Theatre* called "never-before-seen production effects." It also featured, in the words of the *Oxford Companion,* "a long line of choryphees (chorus girls) in what were euphemistically called pink tights but were actually flesh colored."

Despite or perhaps because of a growing acceptance of theater in Indianapolis, Butsch became convinced that a larger theater was needed. He purchased a building under construction at the southeast corner of Illinois and Ohio streets

Ironically, Laura Keene's Combination Troupe was scheduled to move into the Metropolitan for two weeks (late October and early November 1864). Train problems delayed the arrival and limited the engagement to ten days. Three of those days the troupe presented the comedy Our American Cousin, the same play they were presenting six months later at the Ford with the U.S. President in the audience. Keene's career never quite recovered, although she and her players were never implicated in what happened.

17

and changed it into a theater. The original investor had run out of money, and Butsch completed the project, thanks in part to profits he had earned at the Metropolitan.

Though larger than the Met, the new building was similar in that it provided business space on the first floor with two upper floors for the theater. In his 1884 *History of Indianapolis and Marion County, Indiana,* B. R. Sulgrove called it "one of the largest and finest theaters in the West."

The brand-new Academy of Music, according to Sulgrove, would provide a "large and convenient stage" and 2,500 seats. That was a 40 percent increase over the city's first theater structure.

The Academy's opening occurred on Monday, September 21, 1868, just a few days short of ten years after the Met's birth. What newspaper advertisements called a "new" company offered Richard Brinsley Sheridan's comedy *School for Scandal.* Dunn claims this company was transferred from the Metropolitan. Attractions varied from drama to "variety" shows, later termed "vaudeville." Butsch's ownership now involved both facilities, so he was at liberty to make such changes.

The Academy reached a new level of entertainment in January 1869 when it introduced Indianapolis to an actor that the *Oxford Companion* identifies as "beyond question the most popular and respected comedian of the 19th century," Joseph Jefferson. For one week, he starred in the play that had brought him fame and fortune in both London and New York, *Rip Van Winkle.* The second week, Jefferson appeared in other productions, including Shakespeare's *A Midsummer Night's Dream.*

Edwin Booth, brother of John Wilkes Booth, made his first appearance in Indianapolis at the Academy in 1873 for three days with his own company doing primarily Shakespeare. Top price was $2. Booth's elder brother, Junius, and Junius's wife, Agnes, played the theater with more Shakespeare offerings. *Uncle Tom's Cabin* was still selling tickets, and in 1873 its author appeared at the theater for an evening to read selections from her writings.

There were weeks when Academy shows were more lighthearted. Laura Keene was billed as the "Queen of Comedy" when she appeared five years after the Ford Theater tragedy. Tony Pastor (often called the father of American vaudeville) and his troupe appeared three times with an orchestra and brass band. Pastor's initial appearance was panned by reviewers, however, who referred to "obscene jokes" and "slang and pet house wit."

Meanwhile, the Metropolitan (now called a theater again, not a hall, by a new owner), though forced to change its content, continued to have success. Popular music became more prominent, as did dancing and comedy routines. Many a week the stage featured minstrel shows, which had become quite popular. These were shows that featured stylized comic dialogue, songs, and dances usually performed by whites in blackface. Prices were up a bit now to 75¢.

In December 1869, the term *burlesque* turned up in a newspaper advertisement touting a variety show. At this time burlesque meant taking a serious subject and turning it into a comical presentation. However, there were indications that the burlesque of the future was not so far away. In 1871, the Metropolitan featured the "Queen of Burlesque Lisa Weber and her celebrated Burlesque Troupe."

At times one finds ballet listed as part of the entertainment and even trapeze acts. Some advertisements reassured moral skeptics about stage presentations: in a show that featured Mademoiselle Cerito, there was a reference to the "elegant and chaste dancing of this lady." Another week, male and female aerialists were featured as "making leaps from gallery [balcony] to the stage." By March 1875, the Metropolitan was calling its entertainers members of a vaudeville company. Confident this success would continue, the ownership moved forward.

Before 1875 ended, the Metropolitan was physically improved at a cost of $25,000. Among the improvements: a greatly enlarged stage, which involved tearing down a frame building, new seats, and extensive backstage and office alterations. By this time Simon McCarthy owned the building and pledged his place would reopen as a first-class theater.

Theater competition was not limited to the Met and the Academy in the 1860s. Two other downtown outlets (altered for entertainment) were the most prominent with advertisements appearing in the daily press. Masonic Hall was offering various attractions, including "General Tom Thumb and his beautiful little wife," former circus performers for P. T. Barnum, and magician Herrmann the Great. In 1867 it increased its seating capacity to 1,000.

Morrison Opera House opened in 1867, offering variety shows, minstrels, and, at one point, Signor Blitz, "world renowned magician and ventriloquist with his inimitable troupe of 100 learned canary birds." It also could reach out to local talent with a production titled *The Great Rebellion* with 200 teachers and pupils from the city's schools appearing onstage.

Theater activity continued to advance in Indianapolis by 1875 when it was decided it was time for another theater. This would mean three full-time theaters. An enemy of the time, however, would alter the picture within sixteen months after that third theater, the Grand Opera House, opened.

• • • • • • • • • • • • • •

Sometimes a member of these early theater audiences revealed naïveté. One night during the presentation of a then popular melodrama, Under the Gaslight, *at the Academy, one member of the audience just couldn't contain himself. During a suspense-filled moment, as the play's hero was moving about the stage looking for the villain, a man arose from his seat and shouted, "Hey! You damn fool! Don't you see that feller behind that tree?" It destroyed the play's finale, but many in the audience found it amusing.*

• • • • • • • • • • • • • •

19

4

Theater Count Briefly Jumps to Three

Facing. The Grand offered a wide variety of entertainment on its screen and stage for ninety-nine years. Bass Photo Company Collection, Indiana Historical Society.

T he Grand Opera House came on strong. One week before its grand opening, it announced in the local newspapers that it needed 100 young ladies to appear onstage in Grand March scenes in a "spectacular drama." This was an excellent way to remind the city that a new theater was about to open. All who were interested were asked to apply at the theater's box office.

Response was impressive. The spectacular drama, *Around the World in Eighty Days,* was based on Jules Verne's novel, which had only recently been published. (A widescreen film version of this story would appear at the Lyric in downtown Indianapolis eighty-seven years later.) Ads in 1875 described it as a show with "gorgeous costumes and surprising mechanical effects."

The production ran for six evenings and a Saturday matinee during the week of September 20. The theater had opened one week earlier with a melodrama, a story style that had become quite popular with nineteenth-century audiences, emphasizing physical action in its stories. Annie Waite was "supported by an admirable cast" in *Love's Sacrifice* (the play that opened the Metropolitan), followed the next night by a "romantic emotional drama," *Madame Rose.* Miss Waite was the star each evening.

Audiences at the new Grand found a difference in the theater's floor plan. It was located on the east side of North Pennsylvania between Ohio and Market, and it is believed the main auditorium floor was only slightly above street level. With boxes and the gallery, seating totaled about 1,500, as big as the Metropolitan. Chances are the people in charge valued a more accessible audience arrangement. They were brothers James and George Dickson and George's son, Fred. In 1932,

Fred told Darrell Gooch that the Dicksons had been involved in professional theaters all their lives and that they had created an early version of a theater chain
in Indiana and Ohio.

All this experience added up to some attractive bookings. During the first
months there were performances by Julia Matthews's English Opera and Burlesque Company, Mrs. James Oates and her Comic Opera, and Adelaide Phillips's
Grand Italian Opera. There was musical comedy. "Charming little favorite co-

medienne" Minnie Palmer headed up shows with new songs and dances. There were plays by Shakespeare with acknowledged lead players of the time like John McCullough and James Voorhees, as well as minstrel companies and even some weeks of classical music. The Mendelssohn Quintet Club of Boston was an example of that latter category.

Melodramas were frequent, of course. They included more productions of *Uncle Tom's Cabin* (one got a bad review). There were also some weeks that offered the unusual. The honorable William F. Cody (better known as "Buffalo Bill") appeared in a play titled *Life on the Border*. Sex surfaced now and then. Equestrian actress Kate Fisher and "handsome" Jack and his horse Wonder appeared one week, and the reviewer noted that Jack's leading lady "excels in semi-nude parts." When Matt Morgan's "animated art" living tableaux group paid a visit, the *Indianapolis News* reviewer observed that "females were clothed in seductive tights with gauzy scarves to represent apocryphal modesty."

The Grand, frequently listed in ads as Dickson's Grand Opera House, was off to a strong start. Indianapolis was slowly growing into a city that would accept theaters. During the summer of 1875 when the Grand opened, the Academy of Music went into extensive remodeling. By January 1877, James Dickson held the lease on the theater along with a partner, Bob Losey.

Late Saturday evening (January 27, 1877) after the Academy audience had departed, fire broke out between the ceiling and the roof over the stage. It spread quickly to stage scenery and up through the roof, dooming the building. Cause was attributed to a defective flue that extended from the cellar to the roof. Firefighters were delayed in their battle to control the flames because some of the fireplugs were frozen. Within two hours the structure was destroyed. Investors decided not to rebuild.

Meanwhile, the Metropolitan had been providing audiences with limited bookings since the opening of the Grand. In April 1877, it was confronted with problems. On a Sunday (when no theaters were technically open) it provided facilities for a play rehearsal by the Morgan Troupe, which was to perform the following night. The police quickly moved in on warrants sponsored by the YMCA and confronted the management, the theater's musicians, and stock company performers. A trial took place promptly, but it was discovered that charges of desecration of the Sabbath were based on a state law that apparently exempted Indianapolis. Warrants were reissued, based on a city ordinance, and 1,500 people signed a protest proclamation.

A settlement was reached, and the theater scheduled no more Sunday rehearsals. To the surprise of the Metropolitan staff, the *Indianapolis Journal* defended it, but the theater's reputation had been severely tarnished. With the exception of a one-night booking, the theater stayed dark for the next twenty-eight months.

When the Metropolitan reopened in September 1879, it had been enlarged, refurnished, and rearranged. It also had a new name, Dickson's Park Theater. James Dickson had taken over and was reopening it as a high-grade theater. He started out with a sure winner, the popular Joseph Jefferson, who was supported by a "powerful company" presenting his old standby, *Rip Van Winkle*.

Ever mindful of the power of Hoosier favorites, Dickson booked James Whitcomb Riley for an evening of "original character sketches and dialectic readings." Admission was 50¢. Now the Dickson family was involved in both the Grand and the Park, as more and more people accepted the presence of theater entertainment. There was enough business to be shared.

Also still sharing in the growing theater interest in Indianapolis were some of the facilities that had been converted for theater use. By the 1870s, plays and concerts were still appearing in buildings in the downtown area. They included Masonic Hall, Harmonic Hall (formerly Trinity Church), Washington Hall, Mozart Hall, Exchange Theater, and Wright's Hall.

Morrison's Opera House is credited with being the city's first vaudeville theater. It barely made it into the '70s, destroyed by fire.

Amateur theater efforts surfaced early in the city's existence, which no doubt was looked upon with scorn by some of the residents. The Thespian Corps (all male) was the first with the presentation of a farce, *Douglas, or The Noble Shepherd,* in March 1840. Their theater was a former foundry, but some of the actors had prominent names. Although they were credited with providing some "good" plays, the group had disbanded by the mid-1840s.

The Indianapolis Dramatic Society was formed in 1872 and again included some well-known Indianapolis names. This organization presented plays for the next five years, usually for charitable organizations. For the most part the shows were at the Academy of Music. One memorable night, the organization offered a play and some musical numbers. One of them was a cornet solo

• • • • • • • • • • • •

Thomas Edison's "speaking phonograph" was featured at Wright's Hall for one week (admission 25¢) in June 1878. An advertisement stated, "It talks, it sings, it whistles, it laughs!" A reporter for the Indianapolis News wasn't impressed. He wrote that the voice was muffled and indistinct.

• • • • • • • • • • • •

by Athlick Smith. He was to play "The Carnival of Venice" with bass variations. All went well until he got to the bass section. It just didn't work. Erratic squawks caused what Jacob Piatt Dunn described as "a titter, then much laughter, and finally howls and shrieks of mirth." Smith gave it a second try with the same outcome.

More successful was the Dramatic Club. It started out as a club for young ladies in the late 1880s. No men allowed. However, during one of their plays, an actress who was playing a male role lost her mustache in her teacup during a dining scene. Immediately it was decided that it must have members "whose hair would stay on." Men presumably participated in the club's first season, 1890–91. Its longtime home was the Propylaeum.

Was the changing city ready for another theater to replace the Academy of Music? A prominent Indianapolis banker, businessman, real estate operator, historian, and politician thought so, and he made it happen.

Indianapolis was a growing city by 1880, with a population of more than 75,000. It had upgraded its transportation system (streetcars), and more and more retail stores meant more theater customers. Bass Photo Company Collection, Indiana Historical Society.

27

5

English's Opera House
and Its Impact

W hen the state's wealthiest citizen announces he plans to build a deluxe theater in the heart of a city, it attracts attention. This occurred early in 1880, and the city's more liberal newspaper, the *Indianapolis Sentinel,* broke the story.

William H. English became a key member of the Democratic Party, serving in both the state legislature and Congress before moving to Indianapolis from southern Indiana in the mid-1860s. He then launched a business career in banking that produced considerable revenue. By 1880 English was described as a millionaire, and former state archivist Jerry Handfield called him the state's number one millionaire. Handfield researched English for a chapter in *Gentlemen from Indiana: National Party Candidates, 1836–1940,* edited by Ralph Gray.

The English family moved into a home located on the northwest quadrant of Monument Circle. By 1880 some key developments occurred. English acquired the entire property on the quadrant, deciding to build a theater and hotel on it. He then moved to a new residence, and he was nominated to run for vice president on the Democratic ticket. His presidential running mate was General Winfield Scott Hancock, who had acquired fame at the Battle of Gettysburg.

Since political campaigning in the nineteenth century did not dominate one's time as it does today, English managed to travel to eastern cities with his architect. He was seeking guidance and ideas that would make his theater a very special facility. He found what he wanted in New York City at the Grand Opera House, using it as a model. The theater would have its auditorium on the ground floor, still not typical at the time. Seating would include a balcony, and total capacity would be 2,000.

Not everyone was pleased with English's idea. The city's two mainline theaters, the Park and the Grand, continued to be under the same management. In *English's Opera House,* author William George Sullivan accuses them of some active opposition:

> Immediately, the opposition theaters, fearing a new competitor, went into action, enlisting the sympathy of the *Saturday Herald* [a local newspaper]. The *Herald* argued that a town of this size could not very well support two legitimate houses, so why jeopardize business by adding another?

While Handfield calls English one of the city's leading citizens, he also points out a further basis for enmity on the part of others. Following the economic panic of 1873, English foreclosed on many mortgage loans and then turned around and purchased what Handfield calls "acres of valuable real estate at depressed prices during sheriff's sales." Public criticism was not about to stop him from proceeding with his plans, however.

English had a personal reason for building a theater in Indianapolis. He wanted his son, William E., to be its manager. Handfield writes that the thirty-year-old bachelor's lifestyle concerned his father.

Just months before the theater opened, young English had become infatuated with a popular dancer-actress-vocalist, Annie Fox. He could be found in the front row of the Metropolitan during her frequent appearances. He even followed her to some of her appearances in other cities.

Mrs. Fox (she was a widow) apparently didn't share English's ardor. She suddenly married her stage partner. English was devastated. He traveled to New York City,

The city was fortunate to have one of its most prominent citizens, William H. English, build a theater on Monument Circle. Bass Photo Company Collection, Indiana Historical Society.

The senior English wanted his son, William E. English (shown here), to manage the new theater. He was hoping that the responsibility would overcome his thirty-year-old son's philandering. Bass Photo Company Collection, Indiana Historical Society.

31

Noted French actress Sarah
Bernhardt and a highly regarded
American actress, Minnie Maddern
Fiske, refused to accept the terms
of what became known as the
Theatrical Syndicate. For several
years they were forced to play in
tents and modest playhouses in
America. However, in 1906, when
they appeared in Indianapolis,
they were both welcomed to play
at the German House (later
known as the Athenaeum, 401 E.
Michigan Street). Miss Fiske
starred in Leah Kleschna and
Miss Bernhardt in Camille.

Lawrence Barrett was a highly regarded
Shakespearean actor, but one Indianapolis newspaper critic wasn't sold 100
percent. Bass Photo Company
Collection, Indiana Historical Society.

where he confronted the couple on the street and suddenly aimed a pistol at the bridegroom. Annie bravely
grabbed English's arm, heading off disaster. The bridegroom fled in terror.

Three weeks later, the marriage ended, and English
resumed his pursuit. This time he was successful. He and
the entertainer became husband and wife in June 1880
after the family, no doubt with serious reservations, gave
its consent. A honeymoon followed and included efforts
to line up bookings for the new theater.

There is no evidence that English's ever had a resident
company during its early years as did so many of its con-
temporaries. Shows at the new theater traveled with complete casts. By the 1890s, resident companies were history
for the most part, and most of the major traveling productions were acquired by theatrical combines. Daniel
Blum's *Pictorial History of the American Theatre* states
that "powerful managers and theatrical combines found
it more profitable to send complete productions on tour
from city to city."

Indianapolis's newest theater opened with advertisements announcing that "eminent actor" Lawrence Barrett would star all week in a series of Shakespeare classics. He already had local identity, having appeared four
times previously at the Metropolitan. But this visit was
more prestigious. This time he was performing at the
"grand inauguration of this new and beautiful temple of
drama" for the first six days of its existence.

The critic for the *Indianapolis Journal* that opening
night had this to say about Barrett:

> Mr. Barrett's interpretation of the title role [Hamlet]
> is still characterized by the unevenness that has been
> commented upon frequently in dramatic criticisms.
> In depicting the quieter moods of the Prince of Elsinore,
> Mr. Barrett's acting assumes a mechanical air that sug-
> gests a manikin Hamlet, and gives rise to the thought
> that "some of nature's journeymen have made an actor
> and not made him well." However, the reviewer also
> found some favorable moments: "Hamlet's scenes
> with his mother and with Ophelia rise to a height
> of positive genius."

English's theater and hotel were a Monument Circle landmark for sixty-eight years. Bass Photo Company Collection, Indiana Historical Society.

English's Opera House put theatergoing on a higher level in Indianapolis. Its ownership represented prestige and wealth, and it would become a socially acceptable place to be seen. In his booklet, William George Sullivan made these observations:

The finish of the galleries, the boxes and the proscenium arch is of white and gold shaded by a faint cream or fawn color. The carving is of wood and quite elaborate, particularly the entablature [part of a classical temple between the columns and the eaves] and heads of the columns which flank the boxes. . . . The boxes are very showy in their crimson lambrequins [draperies] and lace curtains, and the sweep of the galleries is the perfection of architectural skill.

33

The elegant interior of the city's newest theater was matched only by its remarkable acoustics. Bass Photo Company Collection, Indiana Historical Society.

On opening night the English family members were seen in the left-hand stage box. They retained that accommodation for the next seventeen years.

The first season at English's was a test for William E. It was an on-the-job learning period. Sullivan stated he had something going for him that helped. He was liked by the staff. He also was competitive. During the first years of his leadership he never hesitated to defy his primary competitors, the Dickson family. Criticisms were expressed primarily through his printed theater programs, which included local theater news in addition to cast information and advertisements.

Both theaters came on strong the night English's opened, which also happened to be State Fair week. The Grand offered a new play by James Herne and David Belasco. Herne played the featured role in *Hearts of Oak,* the story of an old sailor who raises two orphans, a girl and a boy, who were not related. The sailor ends up wanting to marry the girl but loses her to the boy. The plot was unusual for its day with no clear hero or villain. The Park settled for a comedy, *All the Rage.* The theater was going after the younger audience with material that was more lighthearted than Shakespeare or Herne's drama.

As it turned out, the heavy competition was to be between the Grand and English's. Both were giving heavy emphasis to the theater tastes of the time: melodramas, minstrel shows, operas, and classic plays (frequently Shakespeare). The most popular drama of this period, however, continued to be *Uncle Tom's Cabin.* During the 1880s many *Cabin* companies appeared at the three mainline Indianapolis theaters. There were seventeen appearances, with over half of them at English's.

Local historian Eva Draegert felt the Grand had the edge in bookings during English's first decade. A review of noted actors and actresses of the time indicate that the two theaters were almost identical in numbers. Many of them appeared at both theaters, though not in the same seasons. Included in the list are Joseph Jefferson, Fanny Davenport, Lawrence Barrett, Charlotte Thompson, Francesca Janauschek, Thomas Keene, and Minnie Palmer.

Young English opened the theater he was to manage despite warnings that the autumn season of an election year was not a desirable time to get strong bookings. English went right ahead. As for the election, the elder English and his presidential running mate, Hancock, lost to the Republican presidential ticket headed by James Garfield. The margin was close, however (a difference of 9,464 votes out of 9,000,000 cast). Fewer than four months after Garfield was sworn into office, he was fatally shot in the Washington railway station, and Vice President Chester Arthur succeeded him.

By the season of 1886–87, competition from the Grand may have been a factor in a decision by English's. On November 28, its Sunday advertisement in the *Indianapolis Journal* announced what the theater called a "sweeping reduction of prices." All seats were affected. The orchestra seats (main floor) were reduced 50 percent to 50¢ as were seats in the family circle (to 25¢), and the seats in the gallery were reduced to 15¢. This competition would continue for another twelve years, since both businesses continued to look for the best in legitimate theater.

Minstrels were still highly popular in the Midwest. These shows provided humor, dancing, and music based on the talents of African Americans. In the words of *The Oxford Companion to American Theatre:* "From the start minstrelsy helped perpetuate the stereotype of the American black: lazy, dumbly guileful, noisy, flashily garbed but essentially happy."

Many of the minstrel companies consisted of white males who not only blackened their faces but exaggerated the size of their lips. Some minstrel troupes used black performers who followed the white man's path and blackened their faces, too. In spite of the racial indignities, these shows introduced fast pacing and

35

Certainly Edwin Booth commanded considerable attention from the learned theatergoers in Indianapolis. In April 1887, the Indianapolis Sentinel announced that a one-day engagement of Booth doing Hamlet at English's had produced the greatest advance sale of tickets in the city's history; in cash it amounted to $3,200, a considerable sum for the time. Tickets were $2 each. Unfortunately, the reviewer for the newspaper felt that even Booth couldn't save the company, which he called "weak." As for the costuming, he wrote they were "abominable in their tawdriness."

played a part in the eventual development of musical theater. They also created some leading black performers. McIntyre and Heath became comedy headliners and appeared frequently at English's. They also launched the careers of white performers. The most successful example was Al Jolson.

These shows paid off at the box office, obviously. Minstrel shows occupied the Grand stage for thirty-nine bookings during the 1880s. That number was lower at English's (twenty-three) and the Park (seven) during the same period. It is unlikely that many blacks were able to see any of these popular minstrel shows. Newspaper advertisements for the Metropolitan theater the week of November 18, 1867, however, carried the following announcement: "A portion of the gallery [defined as the cheapest seats in an upper area of the theater] has been set aside for the exclusive use of colored persons." How long this policy lasted is unknown.

On a higher level, Shakespeare could also gain audiences. During this time all of those productions were limited to the Grand and English's. Lawrence Barrett was the most frequent visitor, with eight appearances; he appeared three times with Edwin Booth at English's.

The word *opera* had a broad definition in the early days of theater. Sullivan states that "opera and theatre were frequently synonymous in the popular mind of earlier days." Many theaters, no matter how small, called themselves opera houses. Going to the "opera" meant going to whatever was offered at the local opera house, which could be anything from burlesque to a minstrel show or a dog and pony show.

In the 1880s in Indianapolis, opera companies narrowed the definition a bit but still offered variety. Seldom did it mean grand opera. It usually meant light or comic opera (for example, Gilbert and Sullivan's *Mikado*). The Grand and English's competed heavily in this category. The Grand featured thirty-nine operas, over half of them identified as comic operas. English's offered twenty-seven opera troupes during the same period with more of an emphasis on Gilbert and Sullivan, mixed with a few classical presentations.

As the acceptance of theaters in Indianapolis grew, so did the popularity of some of the performers. Many of them were touring the country after appearances in Broadway productions in New York City. Charlotte Thompson and Kate Claxton starred in a number of dramas, primarily at English's. Helena Modjeska made numerous appearances at the Grand, twice with Maurice Barrymore as her leading man.

Certainly one of the top theater comic actors continued to be Joseph Jefferson, who made nine appearances in Indianapolis during the 1880s, usually portraying the character his audiences demanded he keep doing, Rip Van Winkle. Six of those appearances were at the Grand, which provided audiences with another popular actor, Nat C. Goodwin Jr., on seven occasions.

The Grand is where the Tony Pastor variety shows were booked. Those continued to be variety shows with music and comics. Pastor didn't allow any material then that bordered on immorality, desiring to cultivate family acceptance of what eventually would be called vaudeville.

Two other personalities were booked by the Grand who no doubt got the attention of the city's relatively new theatergoers: "Buffalo Bill" Cody and the first world champion of bare-knuckle boxing, John L. Sullivan. Cody appeared in dramas purporting to portray his adventures as a Pony Express rider and Indian scout. Sullivan demonstrated his prowess in an act for an early vaudeville company that visited the theater three times.

While the Grand offered considerable competition, English's was the place where many of the longtime stars of the future appeared. These included Jerry and Helen Cohan with daughter Josephine and son George (he would have a long, successful career as a song and dance man). Others were DeWolfe Hopper, comedy vocalist; actress Ellen Terry, known for her beauty and personality; Walker Whiteside, a native of Logansport, who would tour the country with his own repertory company specializing in the plays of Shakespeare; and Eddie Foy, who would be known for his comedy and acrobatic dancing.

In November 1889, the Grand made an aggressive move by introducing its audiences to electrical lighting. This occurred during a three-day engagement of *Little Lord Fauntleroy*, which also was making its first appearance in Indianapolis. Eva Draegert wrote, "Patrons felt that no theater, not even in New York, was more brilliantly lighted. But improvements were needed, for border areas and stage lights were too dim, while the bright auditorium lights were left on during the performance, thus making it more difficult to view the stage." The admission price was $1.

All three theaters were competing primarily during fall, winter, and spring. Traveling theater companies were available for the most part from September to May. With little or no ability to provide comfort during the many hot summer days, the theaters settled for an occasional traveling group. Sometimes these were a bit offbeat.

One summer, English's booked Professor D. M. Bristol's "School of mind endowed, reason-gifted horses, ponies, and mules" for one week. The price was 50¢.

• • • • • • • • • • • • •

Sometimes the Park museum's
headliners were bizarre. One week
"Big Winnie Johnson, one half ton
of flesh," was featured. Another
week there was "Big Elizabeth,
a bigger woman than Winnie
Johnson, with actual weight of
780 pounds and a bust measure-
ment of 118 inches." Another
week there was "M'lle. Christine,
a two-headed living lady with
four arms," followed by the
"9 foot giant, a monster
congo cannibal!"

• • • • • • • • • • • • •

Toward the end of one season, the same theater offered Colonel J. H. Wood's dime shows. Advertisements called this "2 hours of laughter with a giant, comic, a dog carnival, trained birds, roller skaters, and a juggler." There were eleven performances scheduled. After nine of them the theater proudly announced that 15,264 tickets had been purchased.

An even greater variety of the unusual could be found at the Grand during the off-season. Sessions of a state convention on women's suffrage were held there in 1887. Earlier in that decade, the theater booked Sullivan's Hibernian (Irish) Blondes featuring "10 bashful maidens in evening dress." Then there was that time J. Randall Brown, "world-famed mind reader and spiritual medium assisted by little May Brown," held séances one night for "a nominal price of admission." A second session was added two days later, in response, an ad claimed, to the "requests of leading citizens."

The Park was being upstaged by both the Grand and English's during the 1880s, but it had its moments. Three months after the highly regarded French actress Sarah Bernhardt made her American debut in New York City's Booth Theater, she was onstage at the Park. This was during a national tour in which she had a guaranteed $1,000 per performance commitment. How the Park managed that is unknown. However, Bernhardt appeared in a matinee and an evening performance on a Saturday in February 1881. Ticket prices were increased to $3. She starred in *Camille* that day, a classic play with French origins. (Her problems with the Syndicate came later.)

By 1884 the Park was booking early versions of vaudeville. It also added a museum to its facility. For a dime, customers could view exhibits of dwarfs and wax figures in historic tableaux. These so-called attractions were changed regularly just as shows featuring acrobats, dancers, and animals changed their routines from week to week. This was the format at the theater for some five years.

But the big news at the Park in the 1880s was a new technical advancement. Shortly before it removed the museum attractions, it revealed in December 1888 that it had become lighted throughout by electricity, and to mark the occasion it booked a romantic comedy-drama for the week. Electricity soon became a vital part of the city. English's had electricity by 1889. The Grand claimed not only that it was ahead of both theaters but that it was the first American theater to be electrically lighted. That claim is probably open to debate.

Downtown entertainment was expanded before the decade ended with the opening of Tomlinson Hall at Delaware and Market streets. Money came from the estate of druggist Stephen Tomlinson. The massive brick structure opened in 1876 with the first floor housing businesses adjacent to the city market. The second level consisted of a performing hall with a sizable stage and 4,200 seats. It was capable of handling large convention gatherings and eventually basketball contests and bicycle races.

John Philip Sousa drew huge audiences at English's and Tomlinson Hall. Vincent Burke Collection.

Musical events were also booked at Tomlinson. Famed military composer and bandmaster John Philip Sousa and his band appeared there, and years later many of the top black musicians and their orchestras appeared. This was significant because Tomlinson was one of the few downtown entertainment facilities that allowed black citizen patronage.

Historically, the Hall is known for another significant decision. It is believed to be the first downtown site to introduce equipment that could project pictorial movement on a screen. The Grand was the first local theater to take advantage of this new technique as a brief sidelight for its customers, no doubt unaware of what lay ahead.

Changes that widened the audience base had their beginnings in the late 1880s, but many more would occur in the nineteenth century's final decade.

39

The 1890s and
Its Seeds of Change

Facing. Otis Skinner appeared at English's
twenty-four times between 1899 and 1932.
Vincent Burke Collection.

Theater acceptance continued to grow in Indianapolis in the 1890s. The population increased 60 percent from slightly over 105,000 to just over 164,000. The three major Indianapolis theaters led the way in entertainment, but there were changes in what was offered onstage as customer tastes changed and production techniques improved. The new arrangement with Dickson and Talbott meant that all of the city's principal theaters were under the same management. A study of entertainment reveals that the Grand and English's would provide, for the most part, the higher-priced attractions, and the Park would be used to attract an audience that was receptive to lower prices. These theaters would remain together for eleven years.

Many of the leading actors and actresses of the time appeared at the Grand and English's during the 1890s. That distinguished list included Otis Skinner, Richard Mansfield, Robert Mantell, Joseph Jefferson, John Drew, Nat Goodwin, DeWolfe Hopper, Helena Modjeska, E. H. Southern, Julia Marlowe, Lillian Russell, and Walker Whiteside. English's had the edge with additional exclusive appearances by Maude Adams, Sarah Bernhardt, Anna Held, and Ethel Barrymore. Adams was in *The Little Minister,* which had been highly successful on Broadway; French actress Bernhardt was booked twice, appearing in two of what proved to be her most successful roles, *La Dame aux Camelias* and *La Tosca.* Held, a native of Paris, who was discovered by American showman Florenz Ziegfeld, excelled in musical comedy, always flirtatious. She appeared at English's in *The Cat and the Cherub, A Gay Deceiver,* and *The French Maid.*

Ethel Barrymore made the first of many appearances at English's in April 1897. She played a supporting role in *Rosemary*. The leading member of the cast was John Drew (Ethel's uncle), and the play was considered Drew's greatest comedy triumph.

The city's theaters were all moving to more sophisticated stage production techniques in the 1890s. When the American Extravaganza Company moved into English's for three days with *Ali Baba and the Forty Thieves*, the advertisements stated that the show included 200 people, 70 dancers, 700 costumes, and 50 voices. One of the Grand's big bookings during this era was the production of a highly successful Civil War play, *Shenandoah*, while it was still running on Broadway. Another week the Grand offered a $30,000 production of *White Squadron*, claiming it was "a revelation in stage mechanism."

Ironically, the most significant development of the time was introduced to the Indianapolis public at the Park. Dickson and Talbott perhaps decided not to risk what they called "the wonder of the age" at the Grand or at English's just yet. The "wonder" was the Lumière Cinématographe, which projected motion pictures on a screen. This device was rented to the theater at a cost of $100 per day. A private showing was presented on Sunday (when all theaters offering stage entertainment were still closed to the public). The first film presentation (November 30, 1896) was a farce, *A Railroad Ticket*. It got top billing during the week but was just one part of a variety show.

Standing-room audiences at the Park continued for fourteen days. This response encouraged management to extend the novelty six more weeks. One wonders if anyone had any idea of the device's future effect on theaters. One year later, Cinématographe returned, this time to the Grand. It was part of the program for two weeks.

While there were many highly regarded bookings at the three theaters, they were sensitive to broadening entertainment to please varied tastes of potential customers. English's became the home of an early version of the Indianapolis Symphony Orchestra, under the direction

Ethel Barrymore's theater career at English's covered forty-five years (1897–1942). Vincent Burke Collection.

44

of Kurt Schneider. The same theater also booked a week-long engagement of a "Country Circus" that included a parade promoting the show with 200 people and 100 "beautiful" animals.

Both English's and the Grand frequently scheduled wrestling and boxing matches. One week at English's, the boxing champion of Australia, Peter Jackson, appeared. Jackson was willing to fork over $100 to anyone in the audience who could beat him in four rounds. Former world heavyweight champion John L. Sullivan appeared periodically at both theaters, sometimes in a play and sometimes as a vaudeville act.

Indiana's middleweight champion, Charles "Kid" McCoy, appeared at English's during the scorching 1895 summer when bookings were few due to the weather. McCoy challenged volunteers. By autumn, a welterweight wrestling match was booked.

Heavyweight and middleweight wrestling matches took place at the Grand from time to time, and world heavyweight boxing champ James J. Corbett appeared in a play titled *Gentleman Jack* (1893) with "superb scenic effects." Five years later, the same theater offered a film provided by the latest device, a Veriscope, showing Corbett losing his title in Carson, Nevada, to Bob Fitzsimmons. Grand theater ads said the fight would be "especially attractive to the ladies."

James Whitcomb Riley was in demand to read his works onstage. One of the standout evenings occurred in June 1893. The Indianapolis Press Club sponsored an Authors' Reading at the Grand. Besides Riley, there were General Lew Wallace and Meredith Nicholson. Admission was $1.50. The *Indianapolis Sentinel* praised the readings and called the audience "brilliant."

Another Hoosier was listed in a cast that played English's for three days early in 1893. Terre Haute's Paul Dresser was identified in English ads as "a well known comedian" who weighed in at 300 pounds. The title of the play with a railroad theme was *Danger Signal*. There is no record of it ever reaching Broadway. However, a few years later, Dresser was in New York City working for a

· · · · · · · · · · · · ·

One week, the Cinématographe subject matter consisted of the following: Spanish artillery in action; Negro boys diving and swimming; a French lightning-change artist; boxing match; the arrival of stagecoach horses in a parade at St. Petersburg; a Parisian pageant; children dancing; French soldiers reconnoitering; and the favorite of all, babies quarreling.

· · · · · · · · · · · · ·

45

• • • • • • • • • • • • •

In the summer of 1896 the Grand introduced baseball by electricity to its customers. Best seats were 25¢ to see a large illustration of a baseball diamond with lightbulbs indicating what was happening as a game was being played. The home team was the Indianapolis Indians, then in the Western League. The offbeat oddity was booked again the following summer, then faded away.

• • • • • • • • • • • • •

music publisher. It was where he became a highly successful songwriter. His "On the Banks of the Wabash, Far Away" was declared the state song by the Indiana General Assembly in 1913.

New theater competition surfaced in the 1890s with the arrival of the Empire at 138 N. Delaware Street. For the first time the city had a theater with out-of-town ownership. The Heuck Opera House Company of Cincinnati, Ohio, opened its doors for the first time in September 1892. It would operate six days a week with the traditional change of program on Monday. The opening attraction had a solemn title, *The South before the War,* but the show apparently approached the matter lightly. The cast was supplied by the Wallen and Martelle Southern Comedy Company.

The new Empire could seat 1,010 customers and was destined to compete with the Park, since both would zero in on lower priced entertainment. General admission was 25¢, with gallery seats for 15¢.

In its fourth week, the theater booked "Bobby Manchester's Famous Night Owls Beauty Show with 40 Handsome Women, headed by the 'Queen of Burlesque,' Pauline Markham." Although it was not claiming the designation yet, it would eventually become the city's first burlesque theater. These shows featured women in dance numbers and comics. Yet to come to Indianapolis were bump and grind strippers and raunchy dialogue scenes with comics.

Other attractions at the Empire in those first years of its existence included wrestling and boxing personalities, melodramas, and musical variety shows. When a week of vaudeville was scheduled in the mid-1890s, a theater spokesman made a significant observation by way of the *Indianapolis Sentinel:*

> The theater going public is rapidly being taught that vaudeville is one of the true sources of amusement and the days of tragedy and love stories seem to be drawing to a close.

46

The Empire made a valiant effort to maintain vaudeville bookings, but periodically it turned to burlesque. In October 1896, it also showed its customers nine days of moving pictures by way of Thomas Edison's Vitascope. Edison had introduced his device just six months earlier at Koster and Bial's Music Hall in New York City. One scene showed a train coming toward the audience that, according to Kevin Brownlee, caused "some women to scream, others to faint," when it was first shown in New York.

By 1897, Empire ads stressed female cast members. The titles of some of the shows must have been a bit startling at the time: *The Merry Maiden Burlesquers, The Parisian Widows, The Jolly Grass Widows,* and *The Gay Morning Glories.*

Opportunities to see moving pictures in Indianapolis increased as the nineteenth century came to a close. Previous references have been made to appearances at the Park, Grand, and Empire. Moving pictures also were shown one evening at the Fletcher Place Church at a charge of 25¢ and at Tomlinson Hall for a day. At Tomlinson the video included scenes of the inauguration of newly elected president William McKinley.

In the midst of this infant phase of a new entertainment device, the Park was destroyed. Shortly after it had experienced standing-room audiences with its introduction of moving pictures, a fire wiped out the historic playhouse. Only the walls were left standing. It happened early on a Sunday evening (March 7, 1897) when the theater was closed. It was believed the trouble started in the electrical wiring. Low-pressure water service also contributed to the problem. Loss was placed at $100,000 with barely a third covered by insurance.

The fire drew a crowd estimated at up to 10,000, many of them standing on the grounds of the newly constructed statehouse to the west. At one point flames shot high in the air, sending sparks with encouragement from an east wind onto the statehouse grounds. In a rush for safety, several persons were knocked down, the clothing of some caught fire, and one woman was burned on her face. Fortunately, the fire was prevented from spreading to nearby buildings.

Ironically, this unexpected event revealed an insight into the Park's acceptance by Indianapolis citizens. Its initial reception of deep skepticism when it opened as the Metropolitan forty years earlier had changed considerably. The day after the fire, the *Indianapolis Sentinel* noted:

> It is doubtful if anywhere in the United States there is a theater the loss of which would be more keenly felt by its patrons than the Park. Under the management of Dickson and Talbott this theater has been like a home to amusement lovers who have been unable to pay the higher prices demanded by the standard theaters. The same class of people went from week to week to see the different attractions.

Dickson and Talbott immediately assured the city that the Park would be restored and back in business as soon as possible. That happened within five and a half months. The *Sentinel* was ecstatic:

> The patrons of the house will be surprised at the beauty of the place. At the present time it far surpasses any theater in Indianapolis in elegance, convenience, and beauty. There is nothing in Cincinnati that will compare with it and but few houses in the west that surpass it.

Beautification and elegance included a marble lobby and stairways, mirrored landings, and scenic courtyards. Convenience applied to the seating, all of which had unobstructed views of the stage, which apparently not all theaters of that day could boast. Customers were assured of this because the floor had a gradual slope, meaning that the seats in the rear were considerably higher than those in front.

Safety from fire was of considerable importance now, since the city had experienced major theater fires twice (the first victim being the Academy of Music). The Park gallery now had four exits, and customers were assured that the entire theater could be emptied in less than two minutes, a rather daring claim. The *Indianapolis News* had more to say about this subject:

> The architect, Yost and Packard of Columbus, Ohio, says that the building is a slow burning one, so built that a fire could be discovered without difficulty and extinguished before it burned long.

As for the reopening (Monday, August 23, 1897, with matinees daily), Dickson and Talbott obtained the latest version of *Uncle Tom's Cabin* by the Salter and Martin Company. This was considered to be the best of the companies offering the play at the time. It brought fifty people, thirty animals, railroad cars loaded with scenery, three bands, and an orchestra. Bands were used in daily downtown parades, long an advertising device used by circuses.

Prices were increased during the six-day opening. Top price was 50¢ with standing-room-only accommodations in the evening for 20¢. The Park had a busy season once again, concluding the last week of May with a film about the USS *Maine,* which had exploded in the harbor of Havana, Cuba, three months earlier, killing 260 U.S. Marines and triggering a war with Spain.

Competition for the growing theater audience in Indianapolis was beginning to expand. The Dickson Talbott dominance had already been challenged by the opening of the Empire. In the late '90s, a decision would affect the bookings at the Grand and leave traveling Broadway productions exclusively to English's.

As for those motion pictures? Up to now they were considered just a novelty—a novelty that would grow and grow.

1

Theater Enhancement and the Gentle Intrusion of Moving Pictures

Facing. William Sullivan observed of English's Opera House that "as the theater looked on its opening night, so it remained, largely, until the day of its destruction." Bass Photo Company Collection, Indiana Historical Society.

When fire in March 1897 forced the Park to rebuild and add better security measures for its customers, it motivated William E. English to move ahead with plans he and his father had discussed many months earlier. Those plans were to rebuild English's Opera House. William H. English died early in 1896, leaving an estate of $3 million, half of it to his son and the rest to a daughter and her two children. This came some ten years after William E. lost Amy. The talented actress died of what William Sullivan called a "chronic ailment" five years after they wed.

No action could be taken on construction changes for three months (after the Park fire) until the Dickson and Talbott lease at English's expired. The new lessee was the Valentine Company of Toledo and Columbus, Ohio, an arrangement that would continue for many years. Although English went out of state for a new lessee, he looked to his hometown for the remodeling project. The architect was Oscar D. Bohlen, who duplicated an action taken by the elder English when the theater was first constructed. He traveled to New York City to study metropolitan theaters.

Two other local businesses played key roles in the rebuilding. The general contractor would be the William P. Jungclaus Company, with seating and decorative judgments by Charles Badger of the local Badger Furniture Company. The $100,000 alteration included removal of the entire interior furnishings and construction of a new auditorium and stage with the balcony and gallery enlarged. Also added were a number of exits and fire escapes.

Opening night came on Monday, October 25, 1897, with a weeklong appearance of Klaw and Erlanger's "world famed production" of *The Strange Adventures of Jack and the Beanstalk* with a cast of 100. The highest-priced ticket was $1.50.

Sullivan called the accounts in all the newspapers favorable with listings of prominent members of the audience described as "brilliant and fashionable." It was quite a change from the negative views of theater once held by Indianapolis society. As for the performance, it was considered an extravaganza with a host of characters from various fairy tales and nursery rhymes. One reviewer described its star, Miss Madge Lessing, as "a shapely lass . . . trim and rather elegant in her white tights."

On opening night, William E. appeared in the new family box along with his sister and brother-in-law, Dr. and Mrs. Walling, and one of their two sons. The *Sentinel* reported that their appearance was greeted "with a very grateful salvo of applause." The newspaper also noted that the audience demanded Mr. English

• • • • • • • • • • • • • •

William E. wedded again some two
months after his theater reopened.
He and Helen Orr Pfaff became
husband and wife at the nearby
Christ Church on Monument
Circle. They became residents of
the English Hotel, a section of the
theater building. In the spring of
1898, English volunteered to serve
in the Spanish-American War.
Sullivan wrote that at the Battle
of Santiago, "he was twice thrown
from his horse, the second time
the horse falling on him, and the
resultant injuries plus an attack
of dysentery, sent him home."

• • • • • • • • • • • • • •

City historian Edward Leary in an
Indianapolis Star column he called
"Hoosier Scrapbook" (February 20,
1972) claimed that "a great number
of books on the film industry say
that the Phantoscope (a film projector) was first demonstrated
at Richmond, Indiana, on June
6, 1894." Operating the device
was Richmond native C. Francis
Jenkins, who was in Richmond to
attend his brother's wedding. He
and his partner, Thomas Armat,
had created the projector with
film obtained from Edison. Leary's
evidence came from photographs
of clippings from the Richmond
Telegram. Leary granted that other
historians questioned the Richmond date. Edison's historic first
presentation of moving pictures
before a paying audience is believed to have been at a music hall
in New York City in April 1895.

• • • • • • • • • • • • • •

make some remarks at the conclusion of the show, which
he did "with much feeling."

Early in English's second season with Valentine, Maurice Barrymore, father of Ethel, Lionel, and John, would
head a cast presenting *Shenandoah*. The feminine lead
role was performed by Miss Mary Hampton. Sullivan
had this to say about her:

> Miss Hampton is an attractive young actress whose
> costumes, for some unknown reason, were completely
> contemporary and quite Gibson-girlish looking,
> thoroughly out of place.

Again, this was one of those sizable productions that
was not uncommon to this theater. The cast included
200 actors and 50 horses. The battle veteran, English,
was asked to position himself backstage and critique the
combat scenes. During one of these moments, Mrs. English, seated in the family box, fainted. Unnoticed by the
audience, she was removed to her apartment where it is
said she quickly revived.

The rejuvenated English theater with its ability to
handle elaborate scenic and mechanical effects gave it
the edge over its now three main competitors. For example, a native of Centerville, Indiana, Joseph Arthur,
wrote a number of melodramas that involved heavy production techniques. All of these played English's because
the other main contender, the Grand, had a smaller stage
and was unable to handle them. One of Arthur's most
successful plays, according to *The Oxford Companion to
American Theatre*, was *Blue Jeans,* with its locale in Ris-
ing Sun, Indiana, on the Ohio River.

Whether or not stage limitation had anything to do
with it, within a year after English's physical improvements, the Grand changed its policy. The Grand Stock
Company was introduced in the fall of 1898. No longer
would nationally known actors and actresses, traveling
with shows that had been established on Broadway, be
booked at the Grand.

Another factor in the Grand change may have been
the signing of the Valentine Company to handle English's
bookings. The number of stars appearing at the Grand

dropped considerably during the first twelve months after Valentine took over. However, the Grand customers were given a new option of lower prices that accompanied the new policy. The weeklong programs were generally straight plays, frequently identified as society dramas, emotional dramas, or comedy dramas. One in the latter category was *Blue Jeans*. During three of the first four stock company weeks, the theater also offered new Biograph Views, films showing scenes of American military men serving in the Spanish-American War.

War scenes on film played a major role in capturing the interest of theater audiences. At first the idea of pictures showing motion (1896) was a big enough attraction, but when the novelty wore off, filmmakers turned to a greater variety of subject matter. One of the first breaking news stories was a visual report on the assassination of President William McKinley. While Edison was first with such efforts, a book titled *Nickelodeon Theatres and Their Music*, by Q. David Bowers, notes that "Edison was not at first interested in film projection." His Kinetoscope was a device that showed movies for a penny (some historians say it was a nickel) to patrons looking through a peephole. Later he did projected film on a screen by what he called a Phantoscope. Bowers writes that Antoine Lumière and his eldest son studied Edison's devices and made several improvements at a factory in France.

As was mentioned previously, it was Lumière's Cinématographe that introduced Indianapolis to moving pictures at the Park. That action at theaters throughout the country prompted Edison, once a telegrapher in the city's Union Station, to emphasize the projector system. There was the Vitascope, and then there was the Eidoloscope. More and more competition followed. Biograph was introduced by the American Mutoscope Company and was introduced in Indianapolis, again at the Park.

Early in the 1900s, as film efforts turned to story lines, there were those fearless souls who decided that films might be enough to entertain audiences on their own. Small outlets were created. One nickel would gain you entrance, and the term *nickelodeon* was born. Costs were minimal: some rented, some purchased projection equipment. Films became quite numerous, and rentals for them were reasonable.

Indianapolis responded with vigor. The late Charles Eiler, who was intrigued by this era, studied city directories to determine the names and the years when movie theaters (some of them quite small) first came to Indianapolis. He found that twenty-four theaters (some but not all movie theaters) opened in the downtown area between 1903 and 1910 and another sixteen in other parts of the city.

Eiler admitted that "information is very scarce on practically all of the theaters and possibly some of the listings were not motion picture theaters but more on the order of 'penny arcades.'" The Bijou opened February 10, 1906, with moving pictures and illustrated songs. Admission was 5¢. A newspaper advertisement stated that the Bijou would be open daily from 1 PM to 10:30 PM and that the programs were "high class entertainment for ladies, children, and gentlemen." No one yet had banned movies on Sunday, but there was an attempt to do that at the Vaudette, 19 S. Illinois Street. A jury ruled that as long as part of the profit earned on Sunday went to charity, the movie theater's operation was acceptable. Gene Gladson wrote that the Vaudette's operator, Fred Criswell, had testified that part of the profit was given as charity to the Pure Milk Association.

Shortly before the show was to begin on a Wednesday night in February 1910, there was gunfire outside the rear entrance. Adolph Cassau, the second violinist in the theater's orchestra, fired two shots, striking the orchestra's manager, Louis Ostendorf. Ostendorf overpowered his assailant, grabbed the revolver, and fired two shots, wounding the attacker. Ostendorf, described by the *Sentinel* as a well-known musician, died an hour later. He had fired the violinist two days earlier. The show, *The Frolicsome Lambs,* appeared on schedule with its audience unaware of what had happened.

In 1913 the Empire became the Columbia. Advertisements claimed it was offering "clean burlesque at popular prices" and that remodeling had "removed garish decorations." Before it closed in 1923, it took its old name back. One of its final attractions was headed by a young Ethel Waters.

Over at the Park, a popular low price policy continued in the early 1900s with seats selling for 10¢, 20¢, and 30¢. The theater offered a wide variety of entertainment, seldom promoting or booking name stars of the time. Most shows changed at midweek with the same performers. An example of that was the *Behman Show,* promoted as the "finest vaudeville in the world." Its headliners were the Four Cohans—Jerry, Helen, Josephine, and George. George, of course, would become a legendary entertainer and producer on Broadway. The Cohans returned four years later for another visit with George's first musical hit, *The Governor's Son* (this show returned within three months), followed by Cohan's second big hit, *Running for Office.*

During these early years of the twentieth century, the Park was enjoying success. Evidence of this was management's decision to extend its fall-winter season with a stock company that would provide plays into late June. There are many reasons for the great outburst of theater entertainment in Indianapolis. Streetcar lines covered practically every neighborhood in the city, and new interurban service provided those who lived in other towns with easy access to the state's capital. More and more hotels (the Claypool replaced the once fashionable Bates House in 1903) were available along with prominent department stores downtown. The L. S. Ayres and H. P. Wasson stores were thriving before the turn of the century. The William H. Block store would join them and the popular men's clothing and furnishing outlet known as the When Store.

Indianapolis theater researcher Charles Eiler believed that the Bijou,
130 E. Washington Street, was the city's first theater to show only movies.
Further research revealed it also showed illustrated songs when it opened
in 1906. Photo Company Collection, Indiana Historical Society.

Population growth continued, up nearly 65,000 from 1900 to a total of 233,650 in 1910. English's continued to lead the way in professional theater offerings with the Grand and the Park not far behind. The Grand's prestige was enhanced when it eventually made a significant booking decision.

Park seasons included numerous productions of *Uncle Tom's Cabin* and a number of plays and musicals by Hoosier authors, frequently offering them for the first time at popular prices. These included works of George Ade (*Peggy from Paris, The County Chairman,* and *Just Out of College*), George Barr McCutcheon's *Brewster's Millions* and *Beverly,* and Meredith Nicholson's *House of a Thousand Candles.*

More and more the theater began featuring prominent performers, including the Hanlon Brothers' annual productions of acrobats and jugglers, Bert Williams, considered the greatest of black American comedians, and a Terre Haute native, Rose Melville, a frequent visitor with her hayseed characterization in a play called *Sis Hopkins.*

By 1909 the longtime operators of the Park, Dickson and Talbott, turned that affiliation over to the largest theater owners in the country at the time, the Shubert brothers. This new operation lasted only one season. The Shuberts became interested in a brand-new Indianapolis theater, the Murat, which would open in 1910. Another firm, Anderson and Ziegler, would take over the Park.

Into the growing theater mix in the early 1900s came another theater of considerable size at 130 S. Illinois Street. The Majestic contained 1,400 seats with the highest priced seat at 35¢. Its programs included vaudeville and a movie segment.

Later, this theater, which boasted that "sixteen car lines [meaning streetcars] passed by its door," would change its name to the Broadway (1919) and to the Mutual (1926). With the exception of a period of twenty-two months in the mid-1930s, it survived until April 1953.

Competition from the Grand (it had changed its policy again in late 1900, this time to host vaudeville) may have been too heavy for the Majestic. Within six weeks it was offering plays by stock companies.

One of Eiler's listed theaters had a brief life. The Little Gem at 622 E. Washington Street opened in September 1906, but the next day it exploded. The *Indianapolis Star* reported that the "moving picture machine was blown to fragments and the operator saved his life by jumping from the building." This happened thirty-two months after the deadliest fire in theater history occurred at the Iroquois in Chicago, where 632 died. Four days after the Indianapolis explosion, the city council announced it was going to demand better safety measures at all local theaters.

With more and more story lines on film, the theaters began to add mood music, which opened up new opportunities for local musicians. Pianos came first. The bigger the theater and the greater the budget, the more numerous the musicians or more expensive the equipment, as was the case with the pipe organs that eventually occupied a number of the larger theaters. Films at the Vaudette were accompanied by a ladies orchestra.

Rarely during the first years of the new century did theaters specify the content of their films with the exception of news events. Many didn't buy newspaper advertisements, depending on walk-in trade. In 1908 the Manhattan (136 W. Washington Street) became more aggressive and provided titles of two of its films, *Phlegmatic Gentleman* and *Gypsy's Revenge,* in newspaper ads. A week later, the Rex (105 W. Market Street) ran an ad announcing that its film programs were titled *Powers-Goebel Tragedy,* identified as a political drama, and *The Life of Christ.* Lengths of these films are not known, but there was evidence of extending them in the future. By 1910 the Vaudette was featuring films of world heavyweight champion Jack Johnson working out at his training quarters. Ads said these scenes filled 11,000 feet of film.

Some of these new theaters, while stressing their film offerings, added other entertainment such as illustrated songs and, in the case of the Family Theater, provided vaudeville onstage. The Annex (118 S. Illinois Street) offered what it

The Majestic opened in late August 1907, promising it
would provide "improved vaudeville" with three performances a day. It also had a movie segment. Bass Photo
Company Collection, Indiana Historical Society.

called "talking pictures." This was managed by placing actors and actresses behind the screen doing dialogue mouthed by the silent cast on-screen.

Innovations eventually drove many of the nickelodeons out of business, particularly those that had been storerooms, halls, or vacated buildings. Films went
up in quality and price, and audiences were attracted back to the bigger theaters
that could afford to better display this new entertainment.

There was still much activity onstage as the theater choices jumped into high
gear. The Empire, Park, Grand, and English's all had their specialties and were
booked most weeks from fall to spring. Most of the mainline theaters continued
to not offer much during the summer months when electrical fans did only a
minimal job of keeping patrons comfortable.

English's and the Grand Lead the Growing Theater Parade

English's found its niche from the beginning. Book all the prominent talent possible, especially those who are appearing in plays and musicals they have helped make successful on New York City's Broadway. The Grand competed for the same performers for twenty-five years before moving to a specialty all its own—vaudeville. It lowered the ticket price, charging 50¢ for its most expensive seats. Daily matinees cost 25¢. Advertisements now called its entertainment "fashionable vaudeville."

Whether it was fashionable or not cannot be determined all these years later, but it did book some performers who would become highly successful in the future. A young W. C. Fields appeared one week as a headliner in the *Orpheum Show,* which featured seven acts. In a local newspaper review Fields was praised as "an eccentric juggler of much ability who is remarkably deft and clever. He sets off his most serious work with bright and novel comedy." Other performers headed for stardom who appeared in vaudeville at the Grand were Will Rogers, comedian Victor Moore, and a wildly personable vocalist, Eva Tanguay, who would become the highest-paid performer in vaudeville.

National boxing celebrities continued to draw audiences, whether they were still fighting or not. Former world champ James Corbett had retired from the ring and had a new career when he appeared at the Grand. He had become a stand-up comedian with the emphasis in his dialogue on happenings from his worldwide travels. One newspaper critic wrote that Corbett "keeps his audience interested and laughing without a break for twenty minutes."

The theater's most frequent visitor during this period was Gus Edwards. He created a musical act with what he called promising youngsters. Among those who got their first stage experience thanks to Edwards were Eddie Cantor, George Jessel, and Walter Winchell.

Most weeks the vaudeville shows included short film presentations. Toward the end of the decade, when these visuals began to evolve into stories with the stress on comedy and suspense, they became more important additions to the stage acts. This created the need for more theater seats and improved facilities.

Magicians were popular at the Grand. One of the most notable was Harry Houdini. During a Christmas week engagement, he invited the Indianapolis Brewing Company to lock him in a tank of beer. As usual, he managed to escape. Vincent Burke Collection.

In the spring of 1907, the Grand closed. Demolition crews moved in to level the site and replace it with a modern vaudeville house. When the theater reopened in September, the *Indianapolis Star* was most complimentary:

> When Indianapolis theater-goers see the Grand Opera House upon its reopening they will not only witness the inauguration of a new season of high class vaudeville but will discover a rebuilt theater that is handsome, safe and thoroughly up to date with all the modern improvements and conveniences known to twentieth-century theater buildings. . . . There is plenty of room in the new amusement place; the capacity of the main floor is considerably greater than was that of the old Grand, and the handsome new balcony and gallery are vast improvements over the old.

63

Ironically, thirty-three months later (June 1910) the theater's owner, the Anderson-Ziegler Company, announced it was retiring from the field of vaudeville. It sold the Grand and all its other theatrical holdings in the Midwest to George B.

Cox, president of the Cincinnati Trust Company. One month later, Cox sold half of his new holdings to the B. F. Keith Company.

English's moved into the twentieth century with an emphasis on humor. It continued to book shows that had been highly successful on Broadway, and many of them brought laughter and joy. During the century's first decade, nearly 400 such shows appeared here, some of them brought back for a second or third time. Half of them revolved around music.

George M. Cohan's shows always guaranteed good houses, including *The Talk of New York, George Washington Jr., Little Johnny Jones,* and *45 Minutes from Broadway.* Dave Montgomery and Fred Stone were regulars at English's, appearing in early productions of *The Wizard of Oz* and *The Red Mill.*

Individual favorites at English's were growing in number by this time. Eddie Foy and his family were among them, along with Nat Goodwin, May Irwin, Anna Held, and Marie Cahill. Eva Tanguay, who was extremely popular and could get away with singing risqué songs (such as "I Want Someone to Go Wild with

Facing. In 1910, the Grand became the B. F. Keith's theater and was now hooked into a highly successful national vaudeville circuit. Bass Photo Company Collection, Indiana Historical Society.

George M. Cohan (right) with fellow actor Joe Allen led the parade of musical comedies at English's as writer, producer, and performer. He had his father, mother, and sister onstage with him when he appeared in *The Yankee Prince* at English's with a cast of over 100. VanDamm Studio, Vincent Burke Collection.

The Follies played English's year
after year with new editions
each time. English's also featured
an impressive list of performers
who would go on to highly
successful careers on the
stage, in the movies, and on
radio. On the list were Fanny
Brice, W. C. Fields, Will Rogers,
Eddie Cantor, Marilyn Miller,
Ann Pennington, Leon Errol,
and Bert Williams.

Me" and "Go as Far as You Like"), starred in the first *Ziegfeld Follies* to appear in Indianapolis. It was promoted as "Glorifying the American Girl." Producer Flo Ziegfeld Jr. was credited with doing this with dignity.

Comedies were also well supported at English's. Two of the actors who made a number of appearances in comedies were Otis Skinner and John Drew. In the final years of her career, Lillian Russell turned to this category, which became known as comedy drama. Two others who frequently appeared were Julia Marlowe and Maude Adams. Ethel Barrymore was becoming a regular with a variety of roles, sometimes serious, sometimes lighthearted.

Another large category at English's was drama. Melodramas and their extremes of suspense and overacting were beginning to be replaced with more subtle interpretations of the day. Garff Wilson described it as "the movement toward realism in literature which began in the waning years of the nineteenth century and was destined to work great changes in American playwriting."

There was a definite Indiana connection to the newer interpretation of drama, although Indiana author Lew Wallace's *Ben-Hur* had many elements of a melodrama. Published in 1880, the story, which dealt with the origins of Christianity, was heavily read "both in this country and abroad," states Arthur W. Shumaker in his *History of Indiana Literature*. It opened in New York in 1899. It appeared at English's three years later with William Farnum in the title role. It was booked for two weeks, but audience response was so strong that it was extended for an unprecedented third week.

The *Indianapolis Sentinel* praised the ambitious production on opening night (November 24, 1902) and noted that it received "a hearty greeting from a packed house." The *Sentinel* review also criticized its producers, Klaw & Erlanger, for not offering it to Indianapolis audiences sooner:

> There is only one fault to find with the play of *Ben-Hur*. The managers were too long in bringing it to Indianapolis. Here the author of the book resides or at least does

reside many months of the year. He is a stalwart Indianian in every fiber of his being. The play should have had its initial performance here.

Actually, a version of *Ben-Hur* played at the theater for two days in May 1888. However, it consisted of thirty-six scenes onstage, known as tableaux, still a popular method of presentation. People appeared in costumes accompanied by appropriate stage settings and a reader interpreting the significance of what the audience was seeing. Lew Wallace was in attendance. The *Indianapolis Journal* called it "brilliant entertainment." It is not known whether it played elsewhere. Mrs. E. K. Bradford of Washington, D.C., was called the originator who supervised and directed the presentation.

After the 1902 engagement, the epic novel would reappear at the theater three more times with rave notices for its unprecedented production techniques. The *Indianapolis Sentinel* called the mechanical and scenic effects in the play's chariot race scene "a marvel of ingenuity and skill." Eight horses pulling two chariots on treadmills, powered by electricity, created the illusion. A highlight is the smashing of a wheel that enables Ben-Hur to win. It was an impressive achievement for the time. The cast numbered 350.

Another momentous moment at English's occurred nearly six months later when the theater, according to the *Sentinel*, offered the "city's first major stage premiere." It was a presentation of Booth Tarkington's first successful novel, *The Gentleman from Indiana*. Schumaker described it as a "romantic and sentimental novel unlike much of Tarkington's later work."

The "Gentleman" is a graduate of an eastern college (as was its author) who purchases a struggling newspaper in a small Indiana town and achieves success.

Booth Tarkington's *The Gentleman from Indiana* was a best seller in 1900 and a success at English's, but its stage life was limited. Vincent Burke Collection.

67

Above. English's was in excellent health in the early 1900s. Its busiest season occurred in 1907–1908 when it booked eighty-seven attractions. Bass Photo Company Collection, Indiana Historical Society.

Below. The Colonial opened during Thanksgiving week of 1909. At first there was no indication that it would later become the city's most prominent burlesque house. Bass Photo Company Collection, Indiana Historical Society.

The *Sentinel* noted after its run in Indianapolis that "many changes were to be made." Tarkington's future in staging his later novels was indeed bright, but it wasn't apparent in 1905. Another best-selling novel that had a brief stage life was *Alice of Old Vincennes,* by Maurice Thompson. The story was set in the French settled village of Vincennes when it was under British rule. It played English's twice.

Meantime, theater was reveling in the literary output of the state's George Ade. Two of the productions became comic operas, *Sultan of Sulu* and *The Sho Gun.* Three others, *The County Chairman, The College Widow,* and *Artie,* could be called comedy dramas. All were on national tours, and all played English's.

Downtown theater activity in Indianapolis was thriving, but in no way was it peaking. More and more sizable theaters were being built. Thanksgiving week of 1909 saw the opening of the Colonial at 240 S. Illinois Street. Researcher Gene Gladson found these excerpts from the *Indianapolis News:*

> The main entrance is from N. Illinois Street where a corridor in colonial design in marble leads directly to the foyer and the stairway, ascending to the balcony. The foyer is beautifully decorated. From the foyer one passes through a broad entrance into the main auditorium. Its walls are covered with tapestries in restful colors of light gray, pink, and gold. The proscenium arch is beautiful with its elaborate molding decorations which merge tastefully into the decoration of the boxes at each side of the stage.

The theater's management would go after the vaudeville audiences that were keeping B. F. Keith's healthy, convinced perhaps that there were enough vaudeville fans to keep two theaters alive. Six or seven acts were billed each week with daily matinees at 25¢ for most seats and a price range of 15¢ to $1 at night.

Keith's had the edge, however, with more prominent talent and a larger circuit that no doubt could pay better. One exception spotted during the Colonial's fourth week of existence was the appearance of the buxom, brash vocalist Sophie Tucker, who had just appeared in the *Ziegfeld Follies.* Ten weeks later, she returned for another week at the new theater, but apparently the Morris circuit couldn't keep up the momentum. Within two years the theater dropped vaudeville, which had included a weekly film segment, and turned to a resident stock company.

Three stock companies later, the Colonial would attempt to return to vaudeville, with no success, then turn to photoplays, which led to a lease by the Eastern Photoplay Syndicate to provide film programs with admission at 5¢. The Colonial's success was still in the future.

It was a different story when new competition presented itself to English's, but it turned out to be beneficial to a growing city with more and more theatergoers.

69

The Shuberts Come
to Town as the Theater
Competition Grows

Levi and Jacob Shubert booked professional shows for the Indianapolis Mystic Shrine in 1910. Bass Photo Company Collection, Indiana Historical Society.

The Mystic Shrine added a major theater to the city's growing downtown entertainment scene in 1910. The Murat would be a major part of the fraternal organization's new temple.

Wisely, the Shriners made a deal with Levi and Jacob Shubert to run the Murat and book professional shows. They, with their late brother, Sam, had become the biggest owners of theaters in New York and elsewhere. They also produced shows that traveled the country and would now play the Shubert Murat. The Shubert name is long gone in Indianapolis, but the Murat still exists today at 502 N. New Jersey Street.

Architecture was by D. A. Bohlen and Son of Indianapolis, and the challenge was to design a facility that would reflect the Arabic origins of the Shriners. For example, inside the New Jersey Street entrance was a brilliantly lighted foyer with a Roman mosaic imbedded in the floor. It was a Shrine symbol, a camel crossing the desert carrying an Arabian rider.

Above. Marble stairs led to the Murat's balcony, which contained 600 seats. Another 1,155 seats, all upholstered in what was described as "royal plush," occupied the first floor. That floor also provided four double-tiered boxes that seated another 156. Bass Photo Company Collection, Indiana Historical Society.

Below. The Murat's revolving stage made it possible to hold two sets of scenery onstage. Bass Photo Company Collection, Indiana Historical Society.

A novel feature at the time was the revolving stage. It would make it possible for two sets of scenery to exist at one time for theater productions. The stage's equipment was considered some of the best in the country.

Opening night was limited to Shrine members. The public got its first look at the impressive facility the following evening, March 1, 1910. Schubert productions usually were musicals, and one of their typical shows played there opening week. *Havana* starred a veteran "small, red-haired, rubber-faced comedian," James T. Powers. The show had completed two seasons in New York, and it came to Indianapolis (proclaimed newspaper advertisements) with its original cast of 100.

Al Jolson was a frequent musical comedy performer during the Murat's first decade. He made four appearances in a series of shows by the New York Winter Garden Company that always included a "Broadway Beauty Chorus" and 100 cast members. Fanny Brice was listed in the 1912 edition. The company was identified with other musical productions at the Murat. *The Passing Show of 1916* boasted that its cast numbered 150 with a "rosebud garden of girls" on the electric elevated runway. The cast also included a future radio comedy star, Ed Wynn.

One of the earliest of the stand-up comedians was a regular visitor at the Murat. Harry Lauder was described in *The Oxford Companion* as a "wry, wee Scot, who was almost certainly the most popular foreign entertainer in American vaudeville between 1907 and 1923."

The Murat did have its moments when popular music was not involved. One of them was when E. A. Southern and his wife, Julia Marlowe, were onstage. They appeared together here four times, doing works from Shakespeare. Southern was considered to be at the pinnacle of his career during this era. Another Shakespearean actor matched the Southerns in Murat visits. Robert Mantell got mixed reviews nationally, however. Some critics thought his "thundering, roaring" style was outmoded.

The birth of the Murat (competing now with English's) offered Indianapolis a greater choice of acclaimed plays and musicals by nationally recognized professionals. The new theater, however, also excelled in offering more classical dancers, vocalists, and instrumentalists than did English's.

For six years, what Tom Aikins calls "the most significant predecessor to the current Indianapolis Symphony Orchestra" appeared at the Murat. Its conductor was Alexander Ernestinoff. Seats sold for 25¢ and 50¢. These concerts lasted until late 1917, a victim of, in Aikins's words, "a combination of factors, including financial strife and a general anti-German sentiment" due to World War I.

Facing. Harry Lauder was one of many comics who played the Murat. He emphasized his Scottish background and captivated audiences with his Scottish regalia, homespun stories, and songs. Vincent Burke Collection.

Harry Lauder

• • • • • • • • • • • • • •

The great internationally known violinist Fritz Kreisler was scheduled to make his third appearance at the Murat in 1917. However, Indianapolis mayor Joseph Bell issued an order to the theater and to Mrs. Ona B. Talbot, who headed the classical music series, to cancel the engagement. What is difficult to understand is why Kreisler, who was a captain in the Austrian army in World War I, would expect to be accepted in the United States. The mayor was responding to protests that arose throughout the city. The Indianapolis Star of November 21, 1917, carried this partial quote from the Fortnightly Musical Club: "A resolution set out that the members were not prejudiced against the music of the German masters but were unqualifiedly opposed to an officer in the Austrian Army filling his pockets with American gold that might in turn be used to slaughter the sons and brothers of the persons who helped fill those pockets." Years later, during World War II, Kreisler became a U.S. citizen.

• • • • • • • • • • • • • •

The internationally known San Carlo Opera Company of Naples, Italy, visited the theater twice with "20 distinguished European and American artists" who performed such classics as *Aida, Carmen,* and *Lohengrin.* The Boston Grand Opera Company also was booked twice, and there was a visit by the Chicago Grand Opera Company. Prestigious orchestral conductors made appearances. Leopold Stokovsky was at the Murat for a musical festival appearance, and Walter Damrosch conducted a concert by the New York Symphony.

Individual artists were some of the greatest of the time. They included Russian-born ballerina Anna Pavlova, Polish pianist Ignace Jan Paderewski, and two Russian-born violinists, Jascha Heifetz (a teenager then) and Mischa Elman.

The city's newest theater was quite receptive to local performing talent, including a presentation of Gilbert and Sullivan's *Mikado* by Indianapolis Conservatory of Music students, a comic opera by Victor Herbert, *Babette,* performed by students of Indiana University, and a Purdue University *Revue of 1916,* written by George Ade with an all-student cast of 150. In June 1915, commencement exercises were held on consecutive nights for Manual, Arsenal Tech, and Shortridge high schools.

The theater offered *An Afternoon with James Whitcomb Riley,* in observance of the poet's sixty-sixth birthday (October 1915). It included dancers and singers and no doubt some readings by the guest of honor. Nine months later, Riley suffered a stroke and died at his Indianapolis residence on Lockerbie Street. This time it was English's that responded with a weeklong production by the Lockerbie Company, which presented a program of tribute called *An Old Sweetheart of Mine,* the title of one of his many poetry books. Audience response was so substantial that the show, filled with Riley character interpreters, folk songs, and stories, was held over for a second week.

In the city's second decade of the twentieth century, English's continued to be the leader in bringing Broadway productions, usually with the original casts, to Indianapolis. Comedy was the primary theme, some shows with music, some without.

The *Ziegfeld Follies,* filled with feminine beauty, awesome scenery, and numerous comedians, appeared every year and stayed for one week.

Another example of a Broadway-to-Indianapolis talent was the appearance of "doll-faced beauty" and vocalist Julia Sanderson at the height of her popularity. All seven of her stage hits played English's. In one of them, *The Girl from Utah,* she introduced Jerome Kern's popular song "They Didn't Believe Me."

In January 1917, the *Indianapolis Star* carried a story that called Dave Montgomery and Fred Stone "probably the most famous musical comedy entertainers in the world." Just a few days later, they appeared at English's in their latest Broadway hit, *Chin Chin.* Previous appearances of the pair during this decade were *The Lady of the Slipper* and two visits of a musical version of George Ade's book *The Old Town.*

Straight plays continued to be popular at English's, and veteran John Drew still was making the most appearances in this category. He starred in plays with titles like *The Single Man* and *The Perplexed Husband.*

The *Oxford Companion to American Theatre* calls Maude Adams "one of the best beloved of all American actresses." Audiences at English's were invited to see her in some of her most successful roles, all stories by J. M. Barrie, "an author with a barbed wit" (again from *The Oxford Companion*). The plays were *The Little Minister, A Kiss for Cinderella, What Every Woman Knows,* and probably her most famous success, *Peter Pan.*

A number of the actors at English's would end up in Hollywood within a few years, although some would return to the stage periodically. They included Victor Moore, William S. Hart, Ethel and John Barrymore, Nora Bayes, Alla Nazimova, Billie Burke, George Arliss, Ruth Chatterton, May Robson, and Fay Bainter.

In 1910 with the help of newfangled devices such as electric fans, English's decided it would remain open all summer. However, its policy would differ considerably

During a February visit of the Follies of 1915, Florenz Ziegfeld paid a visit to Indianapolis. He was preparing to cast new numbers for a show that would appear in San Francisco in eight weeks and wanted to see where some of his current performers might fit. Indianapolis *Journal* theater critic Hector Fuller asked him how he managed to outdo other musical shows with feminine beauty. Said Ziegfeld: "I have the pick of the market. The average salary of a chorus girl is $18 to $20. I seldom employ any girl, no matter how insignificant her part, to whom I do not pay at least $30 a week. Most get $40, and some of them $50. I have to have girls who know how to dress and behave themselves."

Montgomery and Stone's Chin Chin would be the last of many visits together at English's. They had been partners since 1895 and in Broadway musical comedies since 1901. Montgomery became ill two months after the Indianapolis appearance and died a month later at age forty-five. Stone made his first appearance at English's without Montgomery in January 1920 in a musical comedy titled Jack O'Lantern.

Vernon and Irene Castle were
a husband-and-wife team who
almost singlehandedly created
a rage for ballroom dancing in
America. Born in Great Britain,
Vernon joined the Royal Flying
Corps while the two were appearing on Broadway in Irving
Berlin's Watch Your Step. In
February 1916, Irene appeared
at English's in Watch Your Step
with a new partner. Vernon
came to Indianapolis to bid his
wife good-bye and stayed at the
Claypool Hotel. Two years later,
he died in Texas in an airplane
crash while training American
pilots for World War I.

78

during the warm weather months. It announced that it would provide its customers with "high class vaudeville" and "selected moving pictures" with three shows a day for 10¢. Advertisements didn't reveal specifics.

One film did get top billing in the summer of 1911. The theater announced that it would offer its patrons movie scenes of the Indianapolis 500 (the first one) along with vaudeville acts. Film showings began at 10 AM and ran throughout the day for five days. People no doubt were awed that they could see the race by June 13 (two weeks after it happened) on the theater's "new crystal screen." One week later, it was brought back for another six days.

English's summer season was turned over to two youthful and ambitious local men in 1914. Charles Olson and Benjamin Barton already had opened a major new vaudeville house in 1912, the Lyric, at 133–139 N. Illinois Street, and they owned two other small theaters in the same block, the Isis and the Crystal. Meantime, English's was providing its audiences with some of the first major feature films of the time during its regular seasons. In December 1915, English's offered what it declared was "the world's mightiest spectacle" on film, D. W. Griffith's *Birth of a Nation*. It later would be called a racist interpretation of the post–Civil War period in its portrayal of the behavior of blacks in the South.

Birth of a Nation was booked for three weeks and was extended two additional days. It returned in February 1916 for two more weeks and was back the following December for another eight days. For these engagements the theater called upon its thirty-member orchestra. The top ticket price was $1. Two other Griffith films played English's: *Intolerance,* considered artistically successful but a failure at the box office, and *Hearts of the World,* starring the Gish sisters, Lillian and Dorothy.

Barton and Olson's Lyric Theater opened as a three-a-day performance vaudeville house with short subject movies always included. It contained 1,400 seats (including the balcony), and newspaper stories stressed that the structure was fireproof, consisting of concrete, brick, and steel. The lobby was finished in marble, illuminated

Innovation accompanied the opening of the Lyric in October 1912.
Everyone attending the Monday night premiere was filmed, and they
were promised they would see themselves on the screen the following
Sunday. Bass Photo Company Collection, Indiana Historical Society.

by what researcher Gene Gladson described as a massive cluster of electric lights.
Future patrons were assured that the interior furnishings would be elaborate
throughout the theater.

The city's latest theater offered film programs on Sunday that also included
musical selections. Within a few weeks it was adding vaudeville on Sunday. However, that only lasted a few weeks. The city wasn't quite ready for such activity.

The city's mayor at the time was Lew Shank, who was gregarious, aggressive,
and sometimes controversial. During his first term he closed all the brothels,
campaigned for closing all saloons on Sunday, and supported women's suffrage.
He also saw that there was no unacceptable theater activity on Sunday. Just a few
weeks before his second term ended, he resigned, accused of allowing a streetcar
motormen's strike to happen.

Shortly after Shank's resignation, it was learned that he had signed a contract to appear on a vaudeville circuit. His first appearance (a comedy stand-up act regarding his political life) was on a vaudeville bill at the Lyric. He then launched a twenty-six-week tour that included a week in New York City. Later, he made two more appearances at the Lyric. In 1921 Shank returned to political life and was re-elected mayor with the largest plurality in the city's history. This time he completed his term before returning to the stage. He appeared at Keith's vaudeville with ads proclaiming, "Ex Mayor—now vaude-villian in brand-new comedy offerings." His routine was titled *He Knows His Stuff*. After that, he became an auctioneer and public speaker, and he was planning to run for a congressional seat when he died in 1927.

Former Indianapolis mayor Lew Shank first appeared as a vaudeville comedian at the Lyric. Courtesy *Indianapolis Star*.

Barton and Olson were not afraid to try new ways to attract audiences. The Lyric never closed in the summer. It lowered prices to 10¢ and installed electric fans and an air-filter system for customer comfort. By the summer of 1914 it was managing to run on Sundays again. Bill "Bojangles" Robinson, a "beguiling" black tap dancer, made three appearances at the Lyric, and one week the Three Ink Spots were on the vaudeville bill. This vocal trio originated in Indianapolis and became successful on the national scene.

As more and more movies became available with more and more recognized stage actors appearing in them, the Lyric began showing Paramount pictures with such stars as John Barrymore, Blanche Sweet, Pauline Frederick, Mary Pickford, and Charlie Chaplin. At one point the theater announced it would no longer carry vaudeville, and it closed temporarily to create what it called an "elaborate stage setting for films." It also began referring to its musicians as a symphony orchestra. Vaudeville didn't leave the Lyric for long; it was back six months later.

The Lyric took another turn when it closed for the summer of 1919, only because it was enlarging itself. When it reopened in the fall, it had 2,000 seats and another busy vaudeville schedule. But the effort to operate on Sundays was no longer attempted.

Paralleling the Lyric's policy to show feature movies and combine them with vaudeville, just around the corner at 44 West Washington Street was the Alhambra, believed to be the first theater in Indianapolis built to house only movies. It

The Alhambra was the first theater in Indianapolis built to show only movies. It closed in 1922, eight and a half years after it opened. Bass Photo Company Collection, Indiana Historical Society.

was built by the old Dickson-Talbott chain. It was operating by November 1913 with musical effects supplied by a pipe organ. It provided Indianapolis with a steady diet of feature and short subject films twelve months a year.

Between 1910 and 1919, Mary Pickford was one of Hollywood's most popular silent film stars, appearing in over 100 films. Nineteen of them played the Alhambra during this period. Kevin Brownlow describes Pickford's appeal: "Her films were sentimental, but seldom mawkish. The Mary Pickford character was that of an endearing little spitfire."

The most frequent film visitor at the Alhambra was a lesser-known name, Marguerite Clark. She had a twelve-year career as a stage actress, but left the stage for Hollywood. Twenty-eight of her films played the theater during the teens. Some of the most successful stage actors and actresses of the time who were bringing prestige to the movies were seen for the first time locally on film at this theater. They included Billie Burke, Alice Brady, Victor Moore, Dustin Farnum, May Robson, and Sarah Bernhardt. The same was true of film interpretations of Indiana authors Booth Tarkington (*The Man from Home, Cameo Kirby,* and *The Flirt*) and George Ade (*The Slim Princess*).

10

City's First Movie Palace Enhances Respectability of Going to the Movies

1t happened in the midst of an outpouring of movie houses in Indianapo-
lis. A large, imposing structure was built on the southeast segment of
Monument Circle. It would be called the Circle, and its sign would read,
"Shrine of the Silent Art."

Members included some of the city's most successful businessmen at
the time. The corporation was headed by A. L. Block with officers Robert Lieber,
Meyer Efroymson, and Ralph Norwood. Other board members included Ar-
thur Strauss, Morris Cohen, and Isadore Feibleman. The lone out-of-towner was
A. G. Gillingham of Detroit. The structure was built for $225,000, designed by an
Indianapolis architectural firm, Rubush & Hunter.

During the preparation period, a sizable theater staff was put into place. These
included a managing director, house manager, musical director, and publicity
director along with a technical staff and a house staff that included eighteen
ushers.

Opening night lived up to expectations. All 3,100 of the theater's seats were
filled. Before members of the audience were seated, however, they would encounter the lobby, which the *Indianapolis Star* noted was different from those of the

Facing. Publicity made it clear that the Circle Theater would show only "wholesome" feature films supplemented by carefully selected staff musicians. Bass Photo Company Collection, Indiana Historical Society.

Below. The Circle Theater Company was formed months before its opening (August 30, 1916) to turn a challenging idea into reality. Bass Photo Company Collection, Indiana Historical Society.

"usual motion picture theater" because it contained "handsome and lifelike oil paintings."

And what did the motion picture theater lobby of that time usually contain? The *Star* theater critic said that one usually would find "lurid wild-eyed lithographs depicting impossibly big-eyed heroines and impossibly fiendish-looking villains and impossibly Adonis-like heroes."

The Circle was the first Indianapolis theater to advertise its orchestra. This was perhaps a way to attract the more sophisticated theatergoer. H. L. Splitalny (brother of Phil, who later led a popular all-female orchestra) was a guest conductor. S. L. Rothapfel also conducted. By the early 1920s he would become the highly successful business manager of the Regent Theater in New York City. Edward Resener played in the orchestra's violin section. During an interview years later, he told me that it was a challenge for the musicians because the two maestros made different demands, with one leaning toward the classical and the other favoring more popular musical interpretations. (Resener would become music director at the Indiana, Lyric, and Keith's.)

The appearance of two maestros was not in the original plan. A well-known director and composer, Herbert Stothart, was first choice, but shortly before the opening, he canceled, and panic ensued. Two efforts to replace Stothart intertwined. Both conductors agreed to handle the prestigious position for the week. There was fear that all this could end up in an emotional "explosion." It didn't, but as Resener said, "It wasn't easy, but it did speak well for the musicians who had to deal with it."

Opening night entertainment began at 8 PM with the concert orchestra's overture. It was Victor Herbert's *American Fantasie,* and presumably Rothapfel (later known as Roxy) was handling the baton. Moments later the curtain rose, revealing the theater's stage to the public for the very first time. The *Indianapolis Star* reported that the audience broke into applause "as the beautiful setting of an Italian garden with a soft moonlit effect and with flowers strewn over the stage was disclosed."

Behind all the splendor displayed onstage suddenly came the voices of a quartet singing "Way Down upon the Suwanee River." It was a strange cultural mix, but the reviewers of the day didn't challenge it. Next came the usual dedicatory speeches, followed by the appearance of the screen for the first time. With the orchestra providing musical background, Pathe News provided a review of the week's happenings. The orchestra then took over with a vocal solo by Eduardo Ciannelli. The film feature followed, but not before a "Circle Scenic Study" film was shown along with two more selections by the orchestra.

The feature film at the Circle's opening was titled *Home,* with musical effects provided by the theater's new manual Hook-Hastings organ. One wonders

86

Robert Lieber (upper left, shown with his three brothers) became a key figure in obtaining first-run box office feature film hits for the Circle. Bass Photo Company Collection, Indiana Historical Society.

whether the audience was getting a bit weary by now, but if anyone left early, local newspapers failed to mention it. *Home* centered around a family that comes into considerable wealth. Their good fortune turns all their heads except the leading star played by Bessie Barriscale. Miss Barriscale was in a number of silents and early talkies, but her career apparently was a modest one. The evening ended with a comedy film short, *Skirts*.

Lieber headed the National Films Distribution Circuit. An officer of the Circle Theater Company, he also was vice president of his family's art dealership, the H. Lieber Company.

Adding to the significance of the opening of the Circle is an observation made by the *Indianapolis Star* thirteen years later (September 23, 1929): "At the time [1916] there were in the whole country only two other modern theaters of pretentious size devoted exclusively to pictures, the Strand and the Rialto, both in New York City." More extensive use of the stage at the Circle would come later.

Attractions at the Circle ran seven days a week with a change of program on Sundays and frequently again on Thursdays. Downtown film theaters continued to be exempt from the city ordinance restricting theater use on Sundays. Prices at the Circle were remarkably low during the first years. All seats were 10¢ during the day with three prices in the evening, but none exceeded 25¢. The theater also advertised the fact that it had a filtered air system to ensure comfort during the summer months.

Normally with its First National film connection, the Circle would provide first-run films. One of the few exceptions was *Birth of a Nation,* which was booked for a week well over two years after it first played English's. Prices rose 10¢ for this Griffith epic. More typical were films by stars with First National contracts. They included Mary Pickford and Charlie Chaplin.

Gus Edwards and his young performers continued to be frequent visitors, as were Eddie Foy and his family, the "incomparable ragtime queen," vocalist Belle Baker, and Eva Tanguay, billed then as a "cyclonic comedienne." Newer talent on the circuit, the Marx Brothers, made their Indianapolis stage debut in December 1914 in what was billed as a "ripping musical version" titled *Home Again.* A four-time visitor of this era was Hugh Herbert, who would become an eccentric, not-so-bright film comedian in the 1930s.

Keith's vaudeville shows took pride in providing what it considered "refined" entertainment. In *The Voice of the City,* Robert W. Snyder observes that the "Keith theaters were nicknamed 'the Sunday School Circuit.'" However, there was a week now and then when one might at least suspect that a show might not be suitable for children. In February 1916, the headline act was "The Bride Shop" with "lovable lassies in filmy frocks and lacy lingerie."

Most weeks Keith's included movies on its vaudeville programs, and sometimes they involved current events. In 1912 there was a film report on the sinking of the luxury liner *Titanic,* which struck an iceberg near Newfoundland with a loss of 1,500 lives. In 1917 and 1918 there were World War I films that included the German surrender.

More than two years before the United States entered World War I, the new Colonial offered its customers a film-only program on the war. The presentation, made possible by a photographer for the *Chicago Tribune,* was sponsored by the *Indianapolis Star.* Admission was 25¢, and proceeds were donated to the Belgian Red Cross fund and the *Star's* Santa Claus fund for needy children. Showings ran daily from noon until 11 PM for two weeks.

The Colonial found its niche in 1915 when it went exclusively to photo plays. These were feature films offered seven days a week with a change of program on Sundays, Wednesdays, and Fridays. The theater provided its customers with some rather innovative entertainment during film intermissions. In his *Indianapolis*

Just one street over on North Pennsylvania Street, Keith's was establishing itself as the city's number one vaudeville house. Photographer Ray Conolly.

Theaters from A to Z, Gene Gladson found that "this theater boasted a 'battle of the bands' where two bands were used in opposite boxes. Each band would try to win the most applause from the audience." Interest in motion pictures forced another of the newer downtown theaters to drop vaudeville.

Although competition among the larger theaters was enhanced now that there were nine of them, the eldest of the group, the Park, still survived. It continued to stress popular American drama, melodrama, comedy-drama, and musicals, attractive to an audience that could purchase a ticket most weeks for as little as 15¢. That formula apparently began to lose its appeal by 1910. Longtime owners Dickson and Talbott leased the theater to the Anderson and Ziegler partnership. Changes came quickly.

A popular performer at the Park appeared shortly after the theater's name was restored, and, after an opening performance, he was arrested along with theater officials. Magician Howard Thurston was making his fifth appearance at the theater with his "wonder show of the universe." The show opened on a Sunday. Newspapers announced on Monday that "Managers, actors, and attachés at the Park were arrested by constables for violating the no theater entertainment on Sunday law." Just what happened is not clear, but no performances were canceled, and when Thurston appeared a year later, the show again was to open on Sunday. However, mother nature interfered. A snow storm forced the show to open on Monday.

Periodically feature films were booked at the Park, although stage presentations like *Uncle Tom's Cabin* appeared several times. Eventually the theater signed with a new entertainment circuit, Lyceum, and renamed the theater Lyceum. Bookings included more and more film features. In 1915, the theater showed war films through an arrangement with the *New York Sun*. Sponsored by the *Indianapolis Star* to raise money for a summer mission fund, advertisements claimed that the film was an impartial representation. This, of course, was before the United States entered the war.

Just months before the Circle opened, the Lyceum took a different name, the New Strand, and adopted a format that would be utilized at the Circle. It would feature a house orchestra, vocal soloists, film shorts, and a feature film with the stage as an artistic background. It proudly proclaimed it was the "first theater in the city to do this." Perhaps local audiences weren't ready for this alteration yet.

The theater went dark in midsummer and reopened in the fall as the Park, again with what it called "popular plays at popular prices" at the "home of the speaking stage."

Twice during this decade, all Indianapolis theaters shut down. A critical coal shortage was responsible for the first shutdown on January 16, 1918. This applied also to saloons and other "nonessential places." Theaters reopened at 6 PM two days later. For the next month, one day a week was declared a "heatless day." Far more serious was the influenza epidemic that swept through the Midwest nearly eight months later. Public places throughout the city and state were closed. All theaters were dark October 7–31. The city's civilian death toll approached 350 with another 225 deaths involving military personnel in the area.

Before the century's second decade was over, the fascination with the world of movies had reached surprising numbers in a city that once shunned actors and the theaters they occupied. Eiler provided this information from city directories: 138 more theaters were added to the Indianapolis area (including Beech Grove), and 32

When the Family Theater, 17 Kentucky Ave., opened, it called itself the home of polite vaudeville and later turned to film. Later the Rialto shared the same building and offered stage attractions. Bass Photo Company Collection, Indiana Historical Society.

appeared in the downtown area. Seventeen of these were Air Domes, outdoor facilities, usually adjacent to an indoor theater with shared ownerships. They had relatively short lives due to their vulnerability to the whims of weather.

It was the beginning of the end of the Nickelodeon era. They just couldn't compete with the more established operations that were showing films, too. The Nickelodeon outlets, which had introduced a new invention to many, were outmatched in comfort and equipment capable of coping with a growing industry. In *The American Film Industry*, Tino Balio stated that the Nickelodeon era lasted just nine years, ending in 1914.

Many of the new additions would be known as neighborhood theaters, showing films that had booked previously downtown. These and others included the Irving (5509 E. Washington Street), Hamilton (2116 E. 10th Street), Empress (1122 Central Avenue), Strand (1330 E. Washington Street), Oriental (1105 S. Meridian Street), Tacoma (2442 E. Washington Street), Talbott (2201 N. Talbott), and Tuxedo (4020 E. New York Street). Downtown additions during this period were the Crystal (119 N. Illinois Street), later known as the Isis (113 N. Illinois Street), Royal (16 W. Market Street), Arcadia (459 Virginia Avenue), Iroquois 1 (253 W. Washington Street), Iroquois 2 (432 Massachusetts Avenue), Best (430 W. Washington Street), Pioneer (513 Indiana Avenue), Keystone, later known as the Alamo (150 N. Illinois Street), Starland (113 W. Market Street), Mystic (48 N. Pennsylvania Street), and Owl (444 Massachusetts Avenue).

Seven of the new theaters were on Indiana Avenue. These presumably were available to the growing black population, whose numbers had increased to nearly 17,000 as the city's total population reached 314,000. Blacks were popular onstage, but they were not welcome as patrons at the mainline theaters. It is ironic that Madame C. J. Walker, identified by David Bodenhamer and Robert Barrows as "one of America's first African-American women millionaires," located her hair products and cosmetics company in Indianapolis. The daughter of ex-slaves soon saw the need for an elegant theater where the black population would be welcomed. She made it happen.

Meanwhile, the theater story in Indianapolis would take on other new meanings in the 1920s as the customer choices became greater in number and sometimes a little naughty.

11

The 1920s and the Birth of New Challenges

Downtown theater activity continued in the early 1920s, but there were many challenges along the way. Competition reached a new level with the addition of five new major theaters downtown and twenty others in various city neighborhoods. Six of the latter would be called deluxe suburban theaters with seating capacities larger than the typical neighborhood movie house and stages added for live entertainment. With rare exceptions, their feature films had already appeared downtown.

The first of the deluxe suburbans to appear was the Zaring Egyptian. While noting that "the new theater was Egyptian in architecture," Gene Gladson also found that "huge square blocks of concrete were molded to resemble an ancient Egyptian temple." The Zaring featured a house organist and modest stage productions from time to time.

Seven months after the Zaring opened, the brand-new Uptown was in business. It was built by the Circle Theater Company, and its first week featured Circle organist Dessa Byrd.

Two more of these more sophisticated outlets opened in 1927, the Ritz and the Rivoli. The Ritz opened with an organist and a feature film. One week, early in its new life, it made use of its stage with an all-girl band. A few months later, the Rivoli opened. Built and managed by the Universal theatrical chain, it changed film features four times a week and planned some stage attractions, but the introduction of sound films eventually curtailed that plan.

Facing. The first of the deluxe suburbans to appear was the Zaring Egyptian. Newspaper advertisements claimed that "crowds stormed the opening." An *Indianapolis News* reviewer called it "one of the most beautiful and distinctive motion picture houses in the middle west." Bass Photo Company Collection, Indiana Historical Society.

Above. The 1,400-seat Ritz opened at 34th and North Illinois Street. It claimed that hundreds were turned away. Attractions included an all-girl band. Bass Photo Company Collection, Indiana Historical Society.

Below. When the Rivoli opened at 3155 E. 10th Street, it promised stage attractions, but sound films, still ahead, changed those plans. Owned by a theatrical chain, it announced it would change offerings four times a week. It could seat 1,500. Bass Photo Company Collection, Indiana Historical Society.

The Granada (above) and Fountain Square (facing) both opened during the spring of 1928. Both had a stage suitable for vaudeville, an orchestra pit, and an organ console. Both had elegant lobbies and auditoriums with foreign themes. Bass Photo Company Collection, Indiana Historical Society.

The last two big suburban show houses to be built were just steps apart from each other in Fountain Square, a few blocks southeast of the downtown business area. They opened within a month of each other.

The circumstances leading to these theaters were not coincidental. Gladson found an article in a September 1939 issue of the *Indianapolis Times* that explained it all. The Fountain Square Realty Company was in the process of building a theater when it was approached with a proposal. The proposal came from an unidentified party who was willing to purchase an option to operate the theater once it was completed. When the realty company would not provide the identity of the purchaser, Fountain Square rejected the proposal.

Within weeks someone started building what supposedly was to be an apartment on the opposite corner of the Fountain Square theater site. The so-called apartment turned out to be the Granada Theater at 1045 Virginia Avenue. The previously unidentified owner was the Universal theatrical chain, which also had acquired the Rivoli.

99

The Granada opened first in April 1928, and the Fountain Square followed a month later. Both had a stage suitable for vaudeville, an orchestra pit, and an organ console. Both had elegant lobbies and auditoriums with foreign themes. The Granada was described as keeping with its name, containing "draperies and interior decorations with a Spanish atmospheric design." The Fountain Square's auditorium represented "a large Italian garden under a night sky with twinkling stars."

Lawrence Connaughton (better known as Connie) and his orchestra appeared opening week at the Fountain Square with Connie doubling as the master of ceremonies. He and his group were well known and popular in the city. Also on the stage that week was Mlle. Theo Hewes and her local dance company along with an organist and a feature film. The Granada's beginning was more subdued with an organist and a feature film that changed every few days. However, both the Granada and the Fountain Square eventually went head to head with vaudeville and feature films.

That wasn't the case when fourteen-year-old Nick Longworth went to work for both theaters plus the nearby Sanders (1106 Prospect Street). He recalled that they were all under the same ownership by then. Longworth was what he called the "Candy Man" on weekends. His job was to be sure all candy counters were well supplied. He no longer remembers how much he earned, but he enjoyed the experience, as did many other teenagers in those days. Longworth later served in the U.S. Army (fooling a recruiter because he was only sixteen), spent nine years as a newspaper photographer, and then spent thirty years in Washington, D.C., in a career that exposed him to both the legislative and executive branches of government.

Twelve other small neighborhood movie houses opened in the 1920s, half of them to the north of downtown. Two were on Northwestern Avenue. The Northwestern was at 2462, and six blocks to the north was the Rex. The Broad Ripple was at 818 E. 63rd Street, the Columbia at 2155 Martindale Avenue, the St. Clair, 800 Ft. Wayne Avenue, and the Talbott, 2143 N. Talbott. On the southside were the Arcade, 1909 W. Morris Street, and the Prospect, 2119 Prospect Avenue. To the west were the Emerald, 441 Blake Street, Old Trail, 5760 W. Washington Street, and Princess, 2702 W. Tenth Street. One new theater was added to the eastside. The Eastland, soon to be known as the Emerson, was at 4630 E. Tenth Street.

100   The great outburst of theaters in the downtown area in the 1910s, however, became more subdued by the 1920s. Only six theaters opened, but all played definite roles in the city's entertainment history. By now most theaters were open seven days a week. There had been protests periodically about Sunday showings, but local laws and ordinances were geared to stage presentations.

As theaters began offering both stage and movie programs, previous restrictions just seemed to get buried someplace. The "legitimate" theaters, a term that applied to theaters offering professionally produced plays and musicals onstage, normally were dark on Sunday anyway. That was the lone off day for the traveling casts visiting English's and the Murat.

Most of the theaters already were operating on Sunday in February 1919 when a bill was introduced in the Indiana General Assembly that would legalize this. Proposed legislation gave the final decision to local city councils, who could step in if a theater was showing material considered "lewd, obscene, or immoral." The State Senate approval vote was close. The House overwhelmingly voted yes. Governor James Goodrich signed it, putting it into effect immediately.

Action by the state legislature didn't stop anti-Sunday efforts, however. In April 1922, a committee in Irvington attempted to stop the Irving theater from opening its doors on the Sabbath. A member of that committee was former state appellate court judge Edward Felt (my maternal grandfather). It went to court, but apparently the Irving won the case.

First of the new downtown theaters to open in this era was the Ohio, 40 W. Ohio Street, with 1,500 seats. Its principal owner, Frank Rembusch, also owned the Irving and the Manhattan, 136 W. Washington Street.

The Ohio Theater's addition to the city's downtown scene in 1919 was barely noticeable. But it would eventually stage extremely popular live entertainment, including not one but two organs, an orchestra, and vocalists. Bass Photo Company Collection, Indiana Historical Society.

Charlie Davis possessed all the ingredients to make a pit orchestra a featured part of stage entertainment. He was a likable leader who demanded proper behavior from his fellow musicians both on and off the stage. Photographer Ray Conolly.

Charles Olson and his Central Amusement Co., owner of the Lyric, acquired the Ohio during the summer of 1923. By November Olson added a new concert organ (apparently dispensing with the originals) with Lester Huff playing it and leading a new theater orchestra. Olson's next decision would be even more significant, leading to new popularity. In February 1924, Indianapolis native and University of Notre Dame graduate Charlie Davis and his orchestra appeared at the Ohio stage for the first time.

In his book *The Jazz State of Indiana,* Duncan Schiedt discusses the Davis band's modest but challenging assignment: "While playing the traditional role of the silent film pit band, Davis and his men also were to feature hot music as no local band had yet done. This required constant digging for new material."

The pit band assignment lasted for nine weeks, but Olson assured Davis he wanted him back in the fall. The group spent the summer at Lake Manitou at Rochester in northern Indiana at the Fairview Hotel's dime and dance floor. Davis's group continued to grow in number and always included featured vocalists. Two members left the group that summer and would win national fame in vaudeville and early radio. Pianist Ed East and banjo player Ralph Dumke did a song and talk routine that became known as "Sisters of the Skillet." Both vocalists, they were replaced by Raymond "Cy" Milders, who was quite popular with the ladies in the audience.

Davis became a fixture at the Ohio when he returned in the fall of 1924, remaining there until the summer of 1926, when the group returned to Lake Manitou. Another big decision, this one by the band and supported by Olson, was to feature the now eleven-member band on the enlarged stage with a band platform that could roll downstage on casters.

Meantime, Davis's musicians gained further prestige by appearing five nights a week after their last evening stage show at the new home of the Columbia Club on Monument Circle.

Above. While musical talent was a must in Davis's band, he also wanted his group to participate in moments that required acting in humorous numbers. Sometimes those numbers involved costumes. Photographer Ray Conolly.

Right. Dick Powell was stranded in Anderson without a job when an Indianapolis musician who had heard him sing with a band at a Louisville hotel recommended him to Charlie Davis, who was looking for a vocalist. Powell's long career started at the Ohio. Photographer unknown.

103

Facing. The Apollo was the only key (showing first-run films) in the downtown area that did not have a stage. Throughout the 1920s, it survived with an orchestra, an organ, and featured vocalists. Bass Photo Company Collection, Indiana Historical Society.

Duncan Schiedt wrote about the switch of the Davis format: "This development didn't occur overnight. Davis, though ambitious, was not one to seek the spotlight, feeling less than confident of his abilities as an emcee.... Bassist Dwight Jones was dispatched to Chicago to observe the stage style of Paul Ash, who had initiated the permanent stage band idea at the Oriental Theater, and was enjoying huge success." Once Davis received Jones's feedback, he decided to go with it.

The highly successful Davis days at the Ohio (which always included feature films, newsreels, and a comedy) came to a close in May 1927. Davis and his longtime partner, Fritz Morris, violin and bass player, were invited to take their musical entertainers into the newly opened Indiana Theater after one more summer at Lake Manitou. They accepted.

When Olson lost Davis, the Ohio was never quite the same again in terms of customers. Meanwhile, Olson decided to retire. The Circle Theater Company acquired the Ohio from him, and he sold control of the Lyric and other downtown properties (including four movie houses: the Isis, the Palms, the Bijou, and the Royal) to Ed G. Sourbier. The *Indianapolis Star* (September 4, 1927) described Sourbier's purchase as making him "a dominant factor of theatrical affairs in the Middle West and one of the largest individual owners of important theatrical properties in the country."

Management of the Apollo, which Olson had opened in May 1922, was sold to Fred Dolle and Associates of Louisville, Kentucky. Olson and his wife, having acquired a considerable amount of money for the time, then departed for a worldwide trip. But more future success in the Indianapolis world of entertainment was still ahead for him.

Emil Seidel and his orchestra appeared frequently with either Lester Huff or Ruth Noller at the organ. Later when Dick Powell's effort to make it in vaudeville failed (he had left the Charlie Davis orchestra in 1926), he managed to get vocal booking at the Apollo for six weeks. Eventually, Davis rehired him.

Paramount supplied film features at the Apollo, and Harold Lloyd was one of the more popular comics during the silent film era. His features drew audiences who wanted to laugh heartily, and invariably his films were held over for additional weeks. Other popular film figures on the Apollo screen were cowboy star Tom Mix, leading man Richard Dix, and leading ladies Norma Shearer and Mae Murray.

SCENARIO
RITTEN BY
EORGE ADE

APOLLO

NOW SHOWING
OUR
LEADING CITIZEN

• • • • • • • • • • • •

The Walker Company made its debut in Indianapolis at the Murat in May 1917, offering a summer season of plays, not always but mostly comedies. Frequently the selections had just recently been presented on Broadway. Stuart Walker headed the group, directing and sometimes appearing in plays. The group appeared at the Murat seven summers and then moved to Keith's. The actors varied in experience, but Walker's demands produced professional-level shows. Some of the cast members went on to long careers in movies and television. They included Beulah Bondi, Kay Francis, Will Geer, Paul Kelly, Ben Lyon, Elizabeth Patterson, Charles Sterrett, Peggy Wood, and Blanche Yurka. Cast member Eliott Nugent would become a highly successful writer-actor on Broadway, and Ruth Gordon would enjoy a long career in theater. Gordon's husband, Gregory Kelly, was a highly popular leading man in the company before his death at a young age. Gordon later married playwright-director Garson Kanin. Walker ended up a film director at Warner Brothers.

• • • • • • • • • • • •

Over at the Lyric, vaudeville continued with film shorts playing a secondary role. There was always a headliner, accompanied by six or seven other acts. One week the Georgia Minstrels appeared onstage with their own band and forty entertainers along with five other acts. This group offered four performances a day. Black entertainers were frequent. Buck and Bubbles, billed as the "two ink spots," were a hit with song and dance numbers. Popular music of the day was provided one week by Wen Talbert's "Chocolate Fiends" with a chorus of Charleston dancers.

Entertainment at the Lyric tended to be upbeat, stressing music, dance, humor, and sometimes novelty. An example of the latter was the frequent appearance of "favorite diving star Lottie Mayer and her sirenic sand witches in a series of sensational aquatic feats." Two solo comedians who would become veterans of their trade were Britt Wood, "the boob and his harmonica," and Professor Lamberti, who "lambasts the xylophone." They were still appearing at the Lyric into the 1930s. Music and dancing frequently were headline acts with such titles as *Knick Knacks of 1926*, *Fads and Follies Revue*, and the "spectacular" art review of models appearing in the "evolution of dress from Eve to the present day."

While the Lyric offered vaudeville and films (most of them short subjects) year-round, the more traditional Keith's circuit limited its offerings to the customary fall-winter-spring period during the 1920s. For three summers (1926–28) it booked some entirely different entertainment. This was provided by the Stuart Walker players.

Keith's moved into the 1920s with a format that proved successful in Indianapolis and across the country: six to eight acts of vaudeville each week with film shorts playing a secondary role. Usually advertisements just referred to them as films with no actors identified. There were favorite headliners who showed up every year or so. Ole Olsen and Chic Johnson were in that category. Olsen was a native of Peru, Indiana, and Johnson had grown up in Chicago. This crazy, zany comedy act was popular throughout the Keith's circuit. Other regulars were Rae Samuels, billed as the "Blue Streak of Vaudeville with a new group of exclusive songs," Blossom Seeley, blonde "Queen of Syncopation," and Eddie Leonard, "our laugh friend" and his "minstrel bunch of singers."

There were a number of names in these vaudeville shows that would become highly identifiable a few years later in films and on the radio. They included Jack Benny with his "fiddle and snappy chatter," Edgar Bergen, "the voice illusionist," "popular farceurs" George Burns and Gracie Allen, comics Fred Allen and Bert Lahr, and the Stroud Twins.

In the fall of 1927 Keith's made a significant policy change. It began offering full-length feature films with its vaudeville. It also announced that new shows would open on Sundays, prices would be reduced, and performances would be continuous daily from noon to 11 PM. It also added a new Wurlitzer organ. By November, Keith's proudly announced it was the only theater in the state showing Keith-Albee vaudeville, and attendance was at an all-time high. Two weeks later, more reduced prices were revealed. Nevertheless, Keith's proud vaudeville career would be over in four months.

Downtown theater competition was further enhanced by the opening of another elaborately decorated theater with a seating capacity of 2,600. Loew's State (later Loew's Palace) opened February 14, 1921, with "twenty celebrities of stage and screen" on hand for appearances that first day.

The *Indianapolis Star* raved that "the interior is a masterpiece of plastering which modern improvements have brought to a high state of effectiveness. . . . The seating capacity is one of the most extensive in the city with 1,420 seats in the orchestra (main floor), 100 in the boxes, 108 in the loges, and something like 920 in the balcony." Also included was a new organ console, and within weeks Emil Seidel and his orchestra had become a part of the weekly entertainment.

From the beginning there were shifts in what the theater had to offer, indicating audience response was not living up to expectations. The theater started with feature films and vaudeville. Four and one half months later, it announced it was "departing from vaudeville" and would be booking major photo plays. These included D. W. Griffith's *Way Down East* for the first time at popular prices and films featuring Gloria Swanson, Rudolph Valentino, Douglas Fairbanks, and Mary Pickford, supplemented by musical presentations. It closed for much of the summer for "interior renovation." Early in 1922, prices were lowered again. By the time it observed its first birthday it was turning the management of the theater over to United Theaters Corporation, a subsidiary of the Keith-Albee vaudeville circuit. That meant it eventually would go back to its original format, feature films and vaudeville.

Loew's State came on strong in the 1920s with big production numbers featuring elegantly dressed chorus line members in physically challenging dance numbers. Bass Photo Company Collection, Indiana Historical Society.

Keith-Albee had enough acts working for it that there was no problem with avoiding duplication with the city's Keith Theater. Evidence, however, that Loew's Palace (now) was struggling can be seen in a decision to close for the summer for "redecoration" purposes. It remained dark for seven months, and when it reopened in March 1928, Loew's, Inc., was back in control. It had another highly promoted opening with Emil Seidel and his concert orchestra and Lester Huff at the new Wurlitzer organ. Programs included major film features and star-studded stage productions. The theater had turned the corner and was headed for success.

The theater that would return to burlesque by the 1930s, the Colonial, showed no hint of doing that in the 1920s. It concentrated on providing its customers with first-run feature films that were booked for a full week. Live music was a part of the regular program, with house vocalists and instrumentalists featured. The American Harmonists appeared for a number of years, and for a while instrumentalists were replaced by an orchestra. Suddenly in January 1927 the theater announced a new policy that brought tabloid musical shows (miniature musical comedies) onstage with film features. This lasted seven weeks. The Colonial was in trouble. It closed, and it was revealed it had gone into receivership, but it was only temporary. By mid-April it had been acquired by the Capitol Amusement Co. and had booked Myron Schulz and his Golden Peacock Orchestra along with movies. Once again the anticipated response was insufficient. Within five months the Colonial scheduled a resident stock company known as the Berkell Players. A few months later it was back with movies and musical stage productions.

The busy, highly competitive theater scene of this decade also included six other downtown theaters: two were "old-timers," two were relatively new, and two were born in the period's final years.

• • • • • • • • • • • • • •

Loew's State was one of the first theaters to feature an orchestra onstage as part of its vaudeville acts. The Vincent Lopez Orchestra was earning identity by those who owned radio crystal sets. A few years later, traveling orchestras would be featured frequently on local stages.

• • • • • • • • • • • • • •

109

The Silent Film Era's Finale

Although the city's oldest theater claimed in the summer of 1917 that it had enjoyed one of its most successful seasons, within two years it would make a drastic entertainment policy change. It came in August 1919, after the Park had been closed for two months. The opening stage attraction was called a "musical extravaganza and a chorus of 20 charming beauties." Whether the theater wanted to admit it or not, it had become a burlesque house.

Other Park show titles displayed in daily newspaper advertisements included *The Mischief Makers; Grown Up Babies; The Tempters; Girls, Girls, Girls;* and *Naughty Naughty with a Big Chorus of Lovely Michigan Peaches*. Finally, in late November 1922, when the theater changed management, it admitted it was the "home of Columbia shows with brilliant musical burlesk," as the ad spelled the latter term. Months later, it shed its historic name and became the Capitol.

By 1925, the theater, under new management again, struggled with films and vaudeville, closed its doors for a while, and finished its life with second-run double sound features. Central Amusement Company, headed by Carl Niesse, attempted to save it in 1934, but by midyear its life was over.

Theater survival was not easy for most of the downtown outlets in the 1920s. Even the prestigious English's and Murat had new challenges. Traveling Broadway shows, especially musicals, required ticket prices as high as $2.50. Film theaters, even the Circle, rarely exceeded 50¢ a ticket. Toward the end of the decade, when sound films entered the scene along with a major economic depression, the matter became more complex.

In 1920 and 1921, English's and the Murat provided their audiences with sixty-six musical shows. Highlights at the Murat were two bookings of Al Jolson in *Sinbad*, two appearances of what was billed as "the hit of the century," *Irene*, and annual appearances of the New York Winter Garden Revue with casts that numbered as many as 150. English's matched this with annual visits by the *Ziegfeld Follies*, two musicals with Fred Stone, *Jack O'Lantern* and *Tip Top*, the latter with a cast of 100, and *Apple Blossoms*, with singer John Charles Thomas and dancers Fred and Adele Astaire.

In 1922 the numbers dropped dramatically. Each theater provided ten musical offerings, and English's closed its doors for six months (late March to late September). In August it was reported that the two syndicates operating the theaters had pooled their interests and would no longer compete for bookings. Those syndicates were the Shuberts at the Murat and Erlanger at English's. Speculation arose as to whether English's would remain closed or at the most would play the comedies and dramas, while the Murat would offer the larger shows—larger meaning shows with sizable casts and more technically sophisticated requirements.

One thing had appeared certain: the Murat would continue to book the popular Stuart Walker Stock Company players during the summer. That arrangement had begun in 1917, but even Walker was gone after the summer of '23. The following summer, the theater hired the Indianapolis Stock Company. It provided such prominent local names as Walter Vonnegut, the director, and Marjorie Vonnegut, one of the company's leading actresses. The Walker group returned in 1926 for three more summers, but this time at Keith's.

The no-compete plan involving Erlanger and Shubert in the winter seasons lasted three years, with both theaters offering fewer bookings due to the competitive uncertainty of the time. Entertainment policy changes occurred frequently at most of the mainline theaters. In

• • • • • • • • • • • • •

Just a year prior to the joining of the two syndicates, English's had challenged the Murat by booking (in 1921) a rival company headed by a former leading man of the Stuart Walker group. The Gregory Kelly Players opened with Booth Tarkington's highly successful Clarence. Kelly and his wife, Ruth Gordon, would play all the prominent roles in a thirteen-week summer season. Walker no doubt was not pleased, but it lasted just one season. Meanwhile, English's still competed with the Murat in the summer with the Charles Berkell Players, regular visitors for the rest of the decade.

• • • • • • • • • • • • •

113

August 1925, the Valentine Company of Ohio, which had previously managed English's, was back and added the Murat to its responsibilities. Economic conditions now required that one theater would get the road companies and that theater would be English's. However, choices were shrinking because fewer companies were touring.

In 1925 English's offered fourteen musical shows. The numbers steadily headed downward to a total of six in 1929. The Murat offered a slim variety of popular entertainment, but its specialty again would be classical music offerings. During the 1920s, the Cincinnati Symphony Orchestra visited the theater thirteen times with additional concerts by the symphony orchestras of New York City, Philadelphia, Boston, Detroit, Minneapolis, and St. Louis. A long list of individual artists also appeared onstage. They included violinists Fritz Kreisler, Jascha Heifetz, Jan Kubecik, and Mischa Elman, as well as pianists Sergei Rachmaninoff, Ignacy Jan Paderewski, and Arthur Rubenstein. Typical ticket prices for these concerts were $3.

Paul Whiteman and his orchestra introduced a new approach to jazz music, with seven violinists joining some of the most talented jazz instrumentalists, arrangers, and vocalists of the time. He and his twenty-five-piece orchestra made five appearances at the Murat during the mid-1920s. Four of those appearances were concerts, and the fifth was part of a musical show titled *Little Jessie James.* The ticket price each time was $2.50. Composer-pianist George Gershwin was featured at Whiteman's premiere in May 1924.

Other successful moments at the Murat during this era should not be overlooked. There was that week when Eddie Cantor starred in "a magnificent rollicking revue," *Midnight Rounders,* with twenty-eight scenes; the time that Flo Ziegfeld's highly successful Broadway production of the musical comedy *Rio Rita* played the theater; and the time that George and Ira Gershwin's "smart musical comedy" *Oh Kay!* was first seen in Indianapolis.

As the professional bookings at the Murat fell, the theater became more receptive to amateur talent, particularly presentations by college students. Five of Purdue University's Harlequin Club shows appeared there, and four of Indiana University's Jordan River Revues were booked. Three plays with Butler College casts also appeared, and in 1928 when Butler moved to its current Fairview Park site, the Murat scheduled the *First Annual Fairview Follies.* Both Tech (once) and Shortridge (twice) high schools appeared on the Murat stage with their senior plays. The Little Theatre Society presented five of its plays there, including one by Booth Tarkington, *The Wren.* It also offered *Six Characters in Search of an Author,* which it claimed was the first time it had been on any stage outside of New York. A few years later, the Society would become the Civic Theater.

The closing night of a three-day visit by the Marx Brothers ended abruptly when two deputy sheriffs appeared with an attachment order. Two former comedians in their show *20th Century Revue* claimed they were entitled to nearly $1,500 in back salary. The attachment involved the show's scenery and costumes. The performance was canceled, and the audience got its money back. Photo by White Studio, Vincent Burke Collection.

Noble Sissle was a graduate of Shortridge High School in Indianapolis. His father was the minister of the city's largest black congregation, and his mother was a piano teacher. With her encouragement, he became an accomplished pianist and singer. After high school, he utilized his talents by touring the Midwest Chautauqua circuit. That experience netted him enough income to return home and enroll at Butler College, where he wrote a Butler cheer song, "Butler Will Shine Tonight." Eventually he transferred to DePauw and then enlisted in the army, spending fourteen months overseas during World War I. That's where he met Eubie Blake.

116

The Murat and English's did not ignore the movies. However, they were not frequent at the Murat. Six features were booked during the 1920s, starting with D. W. Griffith's *Way Down East* shortly after it was completed in 1921. Its last film was billed as "the most startling picture of the year." Only women were admitted to the afternoon showings of *Is Your Daughter Safe?* Only men could attend the evening presentations. Admission was 50¢. English's was much more aggressive with the 1920 summer season devoted strictly to feature films. Operating in a brand-new projection booth, films included *The Copperhead,* starring Lionel Barrymore, and *Dr. Jekyll and Mr. Hyde,* with Lionel's brother, John, in the leading role. However, the most popular film at English's that summer was a Cecil B. DeMille photo play, *Why Change Your Wife?* It featured Gloria Swanson, and by popular demand it remained at the theater four weeks.

More typically, major films at English's appeared during the regular winter seasons and were looked upon as classics with enhanced symphony orchestras accompanying them. Some of these included Douglas Fairbanks in *The Thief of Baghdad,* Cecil B. DeMille's *The Ten Commandments,* and *Ben-Hur* with Ramon Novarro and Francis X. Bushman, silent stars of the time. But the theater's reputation continued as it kept providing Indianapolis with Broadway shows, many with their original casts.

Shuffle Along was the first show on Broadway that was written, produced, performed, and directed by African Americans. The show ran two years on Broadway and, after a successful run in Chicago, came to English's for a week in March 1923. It returned for a second week in December. Two of the more popular songs from that show were "I'm Just Wild about Harry" (used by Harry Truman in his 1948 presidential campaign) and "Love Will Find a Way."

Although the number of bookings dropped in the late 1920s, the majority of shows at English's were upbeat, many of them surrounded by popular songs of the time. Fred Stone starred in four shows. Comic Ed Wynn ap-

Above. Noble Sissle (left) and Eubie Blake were a vaudeville team before they created their Broadway hit *Shuffle Along*. Sissle wrote the lyrics, and Blake composed the music. They went in different directions after a second show wasn't as successful. Duncan Schiedt Collection.

Right. Sissle formed an orchestra and found a talented teenager, Lena Horne, to be his vocalist. That ended when Hollywood came calling. Duncan Schiedt Collection.

peared in *The Perfect Fool,* a title that he would use in a future career on radio, and the Marx Brothers (four years after their problems at the Murat) appeared for two weeks in *The Cocoanuts* with music by Irving Berlin and dialogue by George S. Kaufman. By this time tickets for such shows were approaching $4, considerably more than the prices offered for films. However, English's offered seats for 25¢ (later 50¢) in the highest point in the balcony, called the gallery. Unreserved seats were available on long wooden benches thirty minutes before show time.

Annual visits by new editions of the *Ziegfeld Follies* continued through 1926, but Ziegfeld also was producing other hits on Broadway. One of them, *Sally,* had former *Follies* stars Marilyn Miller and Leon Errol in leading roles. Show tunes were by Jerome Kern. Another popular musical comedy featured Julia Sanderson and a "glorious garden of girls" in *No, No, Nanette.* Local audiences responded well when English's booked two operettas shortly after successful runs on Broadway. *The Student Prince* with music by Sigmund Romberg appeared three times. Arthur Hammerstein's *Rose Marie* (with his nephew Oscar Hammerstein II writing lyrics) was booked four times.

English's failed to get Alfred Lunt on its stage in his first hit show, *Clarence.* Written by Booth Tarkington, the leading character was described in reviews as a "shy, bumbling young man." His co-star was Helen Hayes. When it played English's, the other co-stars, Gregory Kelly and Ruth Gordon, were well known to Indianapolis. Other Hoosier-related shows included another stage production of *Ben-Hur* with a cast of three hundred, and a musical comedy, *Abe Martin,* based on Kin Hubbard's cartoon-philosopher.

Other bookings of note at English's in the 1920s were the annual appearances of magician Howard Thurston. His "wonder show of the universe" was onstage for a week every single year from 1919 until 1930. Another was the nine-act drama *Strange Interlude,* by Eugene O'Neil. Curtain time was 5:30 PM with a dinner break at 7:40 and the two-hour final act at 9 PM. Top price was $4.40. Balcony and gallery seats were sold out during a three-day run. It returned for a second booking nine months later. The theater showed one of the silent film era's last major productions early in 1928: *Wings,* a World War I epic that introduced Gary Cooper in a brief appearance with stars that included Clara Bow, Richard Arlen, and Charles "Buddy" Rogers.

118   While English's continued to book traveling companies for stage appearances, sound films were having an impact. The Berkell Players shut down their summer season in mid-June. Charles Berkell stated that "talkies were too much competition." At the Murat the Shuberts ended their lease, leaving the theater back in the hands of the Shriners. Bookings became exclusively musical programs, many by local organizations.

Although the Circle would eventually make some entertainment changes, it started the decade highly successfully with the policies that were in place when it opened. Financial support and business savvy were still provided by some of the city's most successful downtown corporate leaders serving the Circle Theater Company. Those leaders still included Robert Lieber, previously mentioned, who had been heavily involved in the early stages of film theater distribution. While there was deluxe seating available for as high as $1.65, tickets for most of the seats could be purchased for 30¢ and 50¢.

Circle customers viewed Charlie Chaplin's first feature film, *The Kid* with Jackie Coogan, and later another Chaplin classic, *The Gold Rush*. Other comedians who turned to features after appearing in early two- and three-reel comedies were Harold Lloyd, Ben Turpin, and Will Rogers, all at the Circle. During these final years of the silent film era, the Talmadge sisters, Constance and Norma, appeared on the Circle screen more than anyone else. Both played heroines, but Constance was more versatile, also handling comedy roles. Between 1920 and 1926, the Talmadges appeared in forty-one feature films, co-starring in two of them. Their careers ended when sound films replaced silents.

Music continued to play a strong part in Circle shows. The director of the theater's concert orchestra enjoyed prestige. He was responsible for making sure the music that accompanied the films was appropriate. This applied to features and short subjects (newsreels, comedies, previews, etc.). No one stayed very long. During the theater's first twelve years of existence, there were eight orchestra conductors. Why is not clear. It is likely they were in demand and had opportunities in bigger cities. Many were from Europe, and all arrived with impressive credentials. For example, Signor Ernesto Natielle was described in advertisements as "internationally famous." Modest Altschuler was identified in the *Indianapolis Star* as the founder of the Russian Symphony Orchestra and "one of the outstanding figures in the American symphony field." During this period the orchestra was gradually enlarged, growing from twenty to thirty-five members.

The Circle was unique in the early years in that it periodically offered locally produced stage shows in addition to film and musical programs. Thanksgiving week of 1921 it offered *The Landing of the Pilgrims* with a Circle ensemble of fifty voices. Another week it offered what it called a "Spectacularama" with the title *A Festival Tale of China*. This production included "singers, dancers, hippodrome features, and a scene filled with feminine loveliness." Alert, courteous, and friendly ushers were a part of the Circle during the 1920s.

Although the Circle was prospering, by the summer of 1924 the concert orchestra was given time off, and visiting groups began appearing that were more inclined to offer jazz and other popular music. Summers became "syncopation

Left. In 1922, the Circle introduced its new $50,000 Wurlitzer organ, which not only would provide some of the mood music for films but would also be used for solo presentations. Within a year, Dessa Byrd was hired to play it. She became a vital part of shows at the Circle and later at the Indiana. Photographer unknown.

Below. Carl Stotts (second from left, upper row) was a teenager when he worked as an usher at the Circle. One night in 1927, a tornado stopped the show. Stotts said some of the patrons became hysterical. Part of the canopy was torn away from the theater. No one at the theater was harmed, but 150 people were injured in the city. Hundreds of homes and businesses were heavily damaged. White River overflowed, causing extensive flooding. It no doubt subjected the ushers to their most severe test. Courtesy Clarence McGee.

seasons" at the Circle. That first summer, Bob and Gale Sherwood and their group of entertainers provided live entertainment for four weeks. The Sherwoods were well known in Indianapolis and ensured audience response. However, stage shows that featured orchestras also drew customers. Groups that played these contemporary numbers were becoming stars themselves through records and a new outlet, radio.

One of the most popular groups to appear at the Circle during the syncopation series was Fred Waring and his Pennsylvanians, a group that not only could provide instrumental music but could vocalize, too. Formed when Waring was a student at the University of Pennsylvania, they so impressed Indianapolis that they were held a second week with a whole new program.

Little by little, popular jazz bands began slipping into the Circle's winter season. Early in 1927, Paul Whiteman (with advertisements calling him the "monarch of jazz") played the theater with his orchestra of thirty-two members. An *Indianapolis Star* review said the vocal team of Rinker and Crosley (it had to be Bing Crosby) "stopped the show."

Members of the Circle Theater Company were not settling for the status quo. They were convinced that the city could use another big-time movie palace with stage productions year-round. With their support, the $1.2 million Indiana theater was constructed at 136 West Washington Street. It would be the largest theater in the state with a seating capacity of 3,500. It would provide first-run film features along with stage shows, a concert orchestra located in the pit area that could be elevated to stage level, and, of course, the brand-new Barton organ.

Entertainment onstage would be handled through an affiliation with the Publix Theater circuit. A theater pamphlet explained that these shows "are created in Broadway—given their premiere showing on Broadway—and sent intact over the Publix circuit that stretches from coast to coast and which comprises eighteen of America's greatest theaters."

• • • • • • • • • • • • • •

One of my favorites during the 1925 syncopation series was Arnold Johnson and his "Merry Musical Madcaps" orchestra. My parents were at the theater on a Friday night seeing that show. Suddenly Mother went into labor. Dad rushed her over to Methodist Hospital. I arrived later that night. The film at the Circle that week was The Marriage Whirl.

• • • • • • • • • • • • • •

121

The Indiana opened with the old Circle system, a symphonic concert orchestra under the baton of Mikhail Stolarevsky. That lasted just three months. By September, Charlie Davis and his Joy Gang had become the house orchestra, combining their many talents to accompany the Publix shows and silent films.

Stolarevsky and the concert orchestra moved back to the Circle. By November, Stolarevsky was gone, replaced by Edward Resener, an original member of the orchestra when it was formed in 1916. Resener was a highly regarded violinist who at times had served as the orchestra's conductor.

The state's largest theater opened June 18, 1927. Indiana's opening night program began with an overture by the concert orchestra, a newsreel, a stage tableau titled *Pioneer Days,* an organ solo, a scenic novelty, and a Publix stage presentation. The feature film was *The Prince of Head Waiters,* starring Lewis Stone. That wasn't all. Charles Lindbergh, who had completed a world's record nonstop flight from New York City to Paris, was there, too. He flew over the city that opening night and dipped his plane's wings in salute. Sound films would soon change the formula, but the Indiana would stay the course the longest in Indy.

Facing. A brochure proclaimed that the city's newest structure "was con-
ceived by Indiana institutions with Indiana labor, although the glory and
grandeur of its Spanish spirit suggests that it might have been built by
King Ferdinand and Queen Isabella!" Much of the lobby area has since
been restored to its original grandeur. Features include the grand staircase to
the promenade overlooking the grand corridor. Courtesy *Indianapolis Star*.

Above. It was the start of a highly popular entertainment era with a
house orchestra playing the lead in filling seats at the Indiana with
spectators week after week. Photographer Ray Conolly.

13

Sound Moves in with a Vengeance

Sound movies made their first appearance in Indianapolis at the Circle nearly fourteen months before anybody else in the area tried it. It was highly publicized, of course, with advertisements proclaiming that "Vitaphone [a device installed on the theater's stage that played recorded discs] will thrill Indianapolis." The process had been introduced nationally just a few months earlier, and Indianapolis was one of only a few cities utilizing it. First National film studios had become a part of the Vitaphone owner, Warner Brothers, by this time.

What the Circle audience saw that first day (March 6, 1927) were short film segments. The first one contained remarks about the significance of the moment from the president of the Motion Picture Distributors and Producers of America. The spokesman was Hoosier Will Hays. *Indianapolis Star* reviewer Vilas Boyle observed: "The voice is clear and easily understandable with each syllable perfectly enunciated."

Three musical film segments followed. First there was Ray Smeck, playing selections on guitar, ukulele, and banjo. Next came Metropolitan Opera tenor Giovanni Martinelli, singing an aria from *I Pagliacci.*

The third and last segment was "black face singing comedian" Al Jolson with three popular songs, accompanied by "his well known mannerisms." The reviewer concluded that these presentations "are enough to convince even the most skeptical that the Vitaphone marks a huge jump forward for the motion picture industry."

The Circle was not ready yet to drastically alter its traditional format. The feature that historic week was a humorous silent film, *McFadden's Flats,* with music provided by the concert orchestra. The following week, organist Dessa Byrd was back with her customary appearance. These early Vitaphone film shorts, which in subsequent weeks would feature the popular Fred Waring and his Pennsylvanians, Vincent Lopez and his orchestra, and the New York Philharmonic Orchestra, were temporarily shelved after three months to make room for the popular summer orchestra syncopation season onstage.

During the summer of 1927, the Circle booked visiting orchestras every week. The concert orchestra took a summer hiatus, and the organ supplied music for the silent film features. Musical groups included Isham Jones and his Brunswick recording orchestra, Ted Lewis and his merry musical clowns, and Waring's Pennsylvanians. Surprisingly, Vitaphone sound segments were not listed again until late October. The winter season (1927–28) combined the traditional with the new element. Features were still silent and were teamed again with the concert orchestra. Stage shows continued, frequently with local talent, along with organ solos by Dessa Byrd and at least one Vitaphone presentation.

In February 1928, the Circle added another first to its list. It offered the public a feature film with partial sound. *The Jazz Singer,* starring Al Jolson, played one week with the concert orchestra still in use. The feature contained four talking and singing sequences. Audiences were impressed, and six showings a day were offered. The theater still was the only one in Indianapolis with sound film capacity at this time. That competitive edge was about to disappear, however, thanks to the Apollo.

Fred Dolle and Associates of Louisville, Kentucky, took over management of the Apollo in April. Dolle closed the theater for five days for redecorating and to install not only Vitaphone but also Movietone, a competing sound system owned by Fox Film studios. Rather than the disc system provided by Vitaphone, Movietone photographed sound waves on film celluloid, a technique that would become a generally accepted sound system.

The Apollo reopened with a partial talkie titled *Tenderloin,* starring Dolores Costello. It was a melodrama set in the criminal underworld. The theater continued booking both partial sound film features and musical segments by Vitaphone and newsreels by Movietone. In May it showed the highly publicized *Jazz Singer,* but it really got the public's attention when it showed the screen's first all-talkie movie, *Lights of New York,* billed as Vitaphone's "supreme achievement." Leslie Halliwell's *Filmgoer's Companion* calls it "a backstage gangster drama notable for little except its continuous nasal chatter."

Certainly not everyone in Indianapolis was ready to give up on silent films. The Sanders Theater in Fountain Square promoted itself as the "home of silent pictures with no squawkies here." Vincennes native Buck Jones, who was a leading silent star in westerns, was quoted as saying he "didn't think talkies would

Leads Skyroom Orchestra

Beginning its summer season tonight, the new Severin Skyroom is to offer the music of Louie Lowe (above) and his orchestra. Complete new decorations and equipment from floor to ceiling, including an Alaskan mural and an outdoor bar, will form a refreshing background for the popular local maestro's band.

Louie Lowe was Dick Powell's replacement at the Indiana. He handled the assignment while attending Purdue. Courtesy *Indianapolis Star.*

entirely supplant silent drama." Hollywood's Louella Parsons, whose nationally syndicated columns were prominently carried in the *Indianapolis Star,* stated, "I do not believe that any of the producers will ever be foolish enough to destroy the silence of the screen by attempting to make a series of 100 percent talking pictures. It would be the height of folly to try and compete with the stage."

Negative reactions to sound films had little effect on box office income at the Apollo. In October 1928, the theater booked another Warner Brothers sound effort, *The Singing Fool,* again starring Al Jolson. It played the Apollo for four weeks, and the theater opened early some days for additional showings. In his book *Shared Pleasures,* Douglas Gomery called it the film that "convinced all doubters" about the future of sound movies.

Just what was being discussed by members of the Circle Theater Company at this stage is not known, but in February 1928, it was revealed that the operating leases of their three theaters, the Circle, Indiana, and Ohio, were to be sold to the Publix Theaters Corporation and Skouras Brothers. Publix, of course, already was known to local theatergoers as the provider of entertainment units seen on the Indiana stage.

At first this did not appear to be a move toward heavier movie scheduling. The Indiana continued with its highly successful house band, visiting entertainment units, organ presentations, and film features. Sound equipment would be added at the Indiana within six months after the ownership change. The Ohio, however, continued with silent film features and Connie Connaughton and his orchestra onstage with varied entertainers, but not for long. The Ohio would switch to an all-film schedule, adding sound in February 1929. As for the Circle, the new ownership arrangement still had the local group running the facility. Ed Resener became music director, and his wife, Dessa Byrd, remained as the featured organist.

In April 1928, the Circle closed for twelve days in readiness for a house band policy of its own, similar to that which the Indiana was offering. Physical changes included new carpeting on the main floor, movement of the film projection booth from the rear of the auditorium to the top of the balcony, and the addition of four stories of dressing rooms. Stage productions were to include a personable master of ceremonies backed by sixteen "beautiful" dancing girls and the orchestra.

With considerable advance publicity, the Circle selected a former film and stage actor, Eddie Pardo, to be its master of ceremonies. A publicist hailed his arrival with expressions of enthusiasm. Pardo was going to "bring a new style of entertainment. He is hailed as a rollicking youth, a peppy, funny singer. He is a star of musical comedy, vaudeville, and the drama."

Frankie Parrish followed Lowe with Davis until the era ended. He had a long career, including time with Abe Lyman and his orchestra. He ended up as a sales executive for radio station WIRE in Indianapolis. Duncan Schiedt Collection.

All went well the first five weeks. The sixth week began with Pardo's *Yachting Party* on-stage and a movie titled *Dress to Kill* with Edmund Lowe and Mary Astor. Something went wrong, or perhaps the management spotted a flaw and wanted to make a change quickly. Gossip claimed Pardo showed signs of having a drink or two before a performance.

According to Dick Powell, in a 1934 interview with the *Indianapolis Star*'s Corbin Patrick, Powell was suddenly invited to watch a Pardo show. His host was Cullen Espy, manager of both the Indiana and the Circle. Powell said they sat together and watched the performance with hardly a word spoken.

Powell departed and headed for the Indiana, where he was appearing with Charlie Davis. That evening as he walked home, he passed the Circle where he found electricians removing Pardo's name from the marquee and replacing it with his. That, he said, was how he learned he was Pardo's replacement.

A handsome male vocalist was a key element of popular orchestras in the 1920s. With Powell gone, Davis brought in Purdue University student Louie Lowe. He had been a summer replacement previously.

129

Lowe was talented and handled the assignment, but completing undergraduate demands and earning a law degree had its restrictions. However, he created his own orchestra and became a regular at the Indianapolis Athletic Club before he began practicing law.

In one of his several visits to Indianapolis after he was doing well in Hollywood in Warner Brothers musicals, Dick Powell said he was quite nervous about suddenly becoming an emcee right in the middle of Pardo's sixth week. Teenager Ginger Rogers was on the bill that week, and Powell recalled her mother helped him gain some needed confidence. Rogers made two appearances with Powell that summer of 1928 and received rave notices. She also appeared at the Indiana. Powell became a hit as an emcee, but sound films did him in temporarily.

The happy Dick Powell Circle stage era ended in mid-September. The success of sound films was too severe a competition. He became a vocalist at the new Indiana Roof and started selling insurance to supplement his income. Eventually he was hired by the Stanley Theater in Pittsburgh, which was owned by Warner Brothers. That led to Hollywood and the beginning of a successful movie career.

When the Circle shut down its stage, the Indiana became the last first-run theater in Indianapolis with a stage band format. The Circle went to a new and improved sound system it called "perfected sound," and its only live entertainment was Dessa Byrd at the organ. That move didn't last long. By 1929 she was back at the Indiana. Loew's Palace closed up its stage entertainment just three weeks before the Circle did, retaining Lester Huff as its organist. It installed sound equipment by the fall of 1928. The Lyric, now operated by the 4th Avenue Amusement Co., continued to offer vaudeville on its stage through the Keith circuit, which had withdrawn from the Keith's Theater. Sound films didn't come to the Lyric until the spring of 1929.

Keith's had few bookings after the vaudeville circuit moved out, and in April 1929 United Theaters of Cincinnati put its lease up for purchase. It ended the decade dark.

While most theaters that had featured stage offerings were forced to cut back on live talent because sound films were attracting audiences and were less costly, the Indiana just went sailing along. Its stage was busy for the first fifty-eight weeks of its existence. When Davis and his band took a two-week break in August 1928 to do some recording in New York City, the Indiana introduced its newly equipped sound system with an all-film program. The change was only temporary. After that, it was sound films and stage productions every week for the next three years.

The seventeen-member Davis band was bursting with musicianship and personality at the Indiana. Titles were attached to their performances and those of the visiting Publix units. They reveal what was appealing to local audiences of the 1920s. Here are a few of the show titles: *College of Jazz, Jazz Derby, South Sea Breezes,* and *Beauty Shop Blues.* Sometimes the band was onstage, and sometimes it was in the pit and made its entrance with the pit platform elevated to stage level.

In *That Band from Indiana,* Davis recalled that all existing house records were broken in the summer of 1930 when Helen Kane, the popular "boop-boop-a-doop" vocalist, appeared. That week the theater offered five shows a day with a top price of 65¢. In the words of Davis, there was "gold in them thar boop-boop-a-doops."

All the humor and charm that were dominant when the Davis group, known as the Joy Gang, appeared before the public were based on definite regulations. Duncan Schiedt, in *The Jazz State of Indiana,* had this to say about that:

> From the beginning, the orchestra was marked by a tight discipline rarely found in Indiana bands. Where the typical leader of the day might overlook some infractions of the rules, onstage and in the pit of the Indiana theater, every sideman knew his chair was secure only as long as he played the "team" game in both appearance and conduct. Excess consumption of liquor or the slightest hint of narcotics would have meant instant dismissal.

Charlie Davis's success as a master of ceremonies was not limited to Indianapolis. In October 1929, Publix, now known as Paramount-Publix, Inc., sent him to the Paramount Theater in New York for four weeks. His band remained at the Indiana. Still later Publix had Charlie accompany one of its traveling units, again without the band.

When Davis left the Indiana in 1931, it was because he and his group had been booked into the Paramount in Brooklyn. For the next ten months the band would appear at one or the other Paramount theaters in Brooklyn and New York.

Meantime, the Indiana turned to its other popular musician, Dessa Byrd. She continued to be featured, as was an orchestra, now back in the hands of Ed Resener. Top feature films of the day were offered along with stage

• • • • • • • • • • • • • •

In a conversation with me in 1977, Davis talked about the showmanship of some of his band members. There was Ed East, whom Charlie described as "a jolly 275-pounder who could sing clever songs and write them as well." Then there was Harry Wiliford. Charlie said he "could get belly-laughs just by walking downstage to take his trumpet solo . . . then play a beautiful, simple melody that would make you cry." One week Ginger Rogers appeared with a Publix unit. Davis said: "It was so nice to watch a beautiful teenager come onstage . . . sing her little song . . . with her baby doll pumps and her tap, skip, and wing like she was again competing in a Charleston contest. We all loved her." Other up-and-coming Publix visitors included George Burns and Gracie Allen, Joe Penner, Ray Bolger, and Bob Hope.

• • • • • • • • • • • • • •

131

reviews, supplied by Publix with a new emcee, Brooke Johns. Then suddenly, the following summer, the theater darkened its stage and turned to films only. It lasted just ten weeks. Publix was out, and another entertainment group, Fanchon Marco, was its replacement. The first few weeks brought negative reviews of the stage efforts.

Matters brightened when Charlie Davis returned from New York ready to do more business at the Indiana. It helped with Fanchon Marco entertainers added to his shows. But it didn't last long.

The second Charlie Davis era at the Indiana ended after seven weeks. Apparently the house band–emcee popularity was over. An economic depression didn't help, but it didn't stop Charlie. When many of his group, including Fritz Morris, with whom he had created the original band, decided they wanted to stay in Indianapolis, Davis formed a new group and headed east for hotel bookings.

Morris would complete his studies at Indiana University and become a dentist. Drummer Ralph Lillard would become chief percussionist for the newly formed Indianapolis Symphony Orchestra. Art Berry formed his own orchestra for local appearances and also played with the Symphony. H. Reagan Carey, who played the clarinet and saxophone, would join the Lyric pit orchestra and end up on the staff of IUPUI. Davis would keep a promise to his wife, Miriam, and retire as a professional musician in 1935. They moved to Oswego, New York, where he purchased a furniture store.

The transitional 1920s also saw a breakthrough for the area's growing black population. By 1930 it would represent over 10 percent of the population.

Madame C. J. Walker's entrepreneurial strategies and organizational skills revolutionized what would become a multibillion-dollar ethnic hair care and cosmetics industry. The Walker Building, a four-story yellow brick triangle building, served as headquarters for Walker's manufacturing company as well as a theater. Madame Walker planned it but died more than eight years before it was completed.

Facing top. On December 26, 1927, the Walker, an Egyptian-style theater with 1,500 seats, opened at 603 Indiana Avenue. It was significant because for the first time in the city's history, a sizable, prestigious theater would be available to the black population. Up until then, their theater options were limited to small facilities in the same neighborhood. Bass Photo Company Collection, Indiana Historical Society.

Facing bottom. Financed by Madame C. J. Walker, African American entrepreneur, philanthropist, and political activist, the Walker Theater offered blacks a movie and a stage show in a well-built, dignified structure. In 1914, Walker learned that the Isis Theater downtown had increased its ticket price from 15¢ to 25¢ for what it called "colored people." That day Madame Walker vowed to build her own movie house. She is shown here at the wheel of a car with her niece beside her and two business associates. A'Lelia Bundles/Walker Family/madamcjwalker.com.

The silent film feature on opening night, December 26, 1927, was *The Magic Flame*, starring Ronald Coleman and Vilma Bánky. Musical effects were provided by Mary Singleton at the "mighty Barton organ." Stage and film attractions were to change twice a week with the most expensive seats selling for 40¢. During those first weeks of musical revues onstage, two standouts were women vocalists. Ethel Waters played the theater for a week, as did Bessie Smith on two occasions. Live entertainment continued to stress music. Here are some of the performers: Mamie Smith and her original Jazz Hounds, Jazz Joy, Hello Dixieland, and Jazz a La Carte. Dancing also was popular, with shows that included the Walker Theater Beauty Chorus.

During the Depression, stage shows became fewer at the Walker Theater, but many of the popular films of the day were booked there. It still would be many years before an African American would feel welcomed at just any theater he or she wished to attend in the Indianapolis area. Not surprisingly, the Walker stopped placing advertisements in the city's daily newspapers. Theater advertisements carried by the African American–owned *Indianapolis Recorder* guided the reader in selecting a theater visit.

There were several theaters available to the black citizen (as strange as that seems today), but in practically every instance, the movies were second-run, meaning they had first been shown downtown. Available movie houses were located in or near black neighborhoods. They included Hill's Indiana at 1414 Indiana Avenue, which sometimes had stage attractions with its films. Others were the Douglas, Lido, Senate, Two Johns, and the Park.

The race policy did not apply to all downtown theaters. The Capitol included these words in its *Recorder* ads: "You are always welcome at the Capitol." Shows at two burlesque houses, the Colonial (later the Fox) and the Rialto, could be found in the *Recorder,* and the Gem, located just across the street from the statehouse, had the *Recorder*'s approval.

Mainline theater ads did appear in the *Recorder,* but not often. When Ethel Waters appeared at the Murat, the weekly carried a front-page story with a picture of the prominent star. Four years later when she returned in another show at English's, ads appeared beckoning *Recorder* readers to attend. However, the many black musicians of the time appeared at Indiana Avenue nightclubs and Tomlinson Hall. All received *Recorder* newspaper attention, and sometimes white customers attended, too. But, of course, all the highly regarded black musicians performed in downtown theaters that the black audiences were forbidden to attend.

Reginald DuValle (with accordion) and his talented Blackbirds, a ten-member jazz orchestra, were on the first stage bill with two other acts when the Walker Theater opened. DuValle's group would become the house orchestra. DuValle has been credited with teaching Hoagy Carmichael how to play the piano. Courtesy of DuValle's son, Reginald DuValle.

14

The 1930s and
Its Challenges

As the effects of the Great Depression spread and the quality of sound on film improved, a number of the city's theaters were confronted with new challenges. Keith's, now owned by the United Theater Company, renovated its building and rented space for public and private affairs. With the exception of two performances of the *Jordan River Revue* by Indiana University students, an appearance by Mlle. Hewes's local dance students, and a twenty-two-week season by the Berkell Players (stressing comedies), the theater was dark for forty-four months. It reopened briefly with a film program that included a feature titled *Fools of Passion*. Only women were admitted, but halfway through the week, only males could attend. The presentations included living models, according to Keith's advertisements.

During the summer of 1933, Keith's reconditioned and redecorated its interior while new sound equipment was installed. It then offered what it called "choice second-run film features." This policy lasted only a few months, and the theater went dark again. The Ohio also offered second-run films, having abandoned its stage offerings in 1928. Within five years the Circle Theater Company relieved itself of the Ohio, surrendering its lease. It was rarely used after the mid-1930s.

During the early 1930s, the Loew's is where local movie fans first heard the voices of Joan Crawford, Greta Garbo, Ronald Colman, Mary Pickford, Norma Shearer, John Gilbert, Douglas Fairbanks, and Robert Montgomery. This also is where Jean Harlow made her Indianapolis screen debut in Howard Hughes's epic, *Hell's Angels;* where the three Barrymores, Ethel, John, and Lionel, were first seen together on film in *Rasputin;* and where Johnny Weissmuller and Maureen O'Sullivan introduced fans to *Tarzan and His Mate.*

During the early 1930s, the Loew's is where local
movie fans first heard the voices of their favorite
stars, including Johnny Weissmuller's now-famous
Tarzan yell. Duncan Schiedt Collection.

In January 1934, Loew's management began reopening its stage from time to time. Its first offering was a *Century of Progress Revue*, featuring what it claimed was the originator of the fan dance, Faith Bacon. The show also included twelve models and twelve dancing girls. Two weeks later, Ted Lewis and his Musical Klowns moved in for a week.

Little did I realize that this was an effort to challenge the Lyric, which was booking vaudeville stage shows weekly. The decision also was timely because the Indiana was dropping weekly stage offerings for the first time. In promoting its new policy, Loew's proudly announced that it was replacing large sound horns for its films with new compact devices that disappeared immediately and eliminated awkward delays when going from film to stage shows. Ironically, after this was accomplished, only four more stage shows were scheduled during the 1930s. Two of them featured the popular Cab Calloway and his Cotton Club Orchestra, which attracted record-breaking audiences. Grandma and I saw both of them.

Many of the most popular films of the time appeared at Loew's: the *Thin Man* series starring William Powell and Myrna Loy; operettas starring Jeanette MacDonald and Nelson Eddy; the many adventures of Andy Hardy, starring Mickey Rooney; and Judy Garland in *The Wizard of Oz*. Some came from classic literature: *Treasure Island, David Copperfield, Tale of Two Cities, Mutiny on the Bounty, Romeo and Juliet,* and *The Adventures of Tom Sawyer.* These were just a fraction of the films shown, many of them as parts of double features.

Another key theater for movie fans was the Apollo. It dismissed all its musicians once sound was installed and went exclusively to films. It ended the 1920s with a box office winner titled *Sunnyside Up,* claiming that it was the first original musical comedy on-screen. Its stars, Janet Gaynor and Charles Farrell, were not musicians or vocalists, but that was supplied by others. The film played four weeks.

One of the most popular film stars was Will Rogers, who played down-to-earth, always wise characters. Twenty-one Rogers sound features were first seen at the Apollo between late 1929 and 1935, the year he was killed in a plane crash. In 1934, the *Indianapolis Star* reported 310,643 people attended the theater to see Rogers appearing in films that occupied fourteen weeks that year. Four Rogers films stayed four weeks; two of them, *Steamboat Round the Bend* and *In Old Kentucky,* were released after his death.

Another top Apollo film star was Shirley Temple, who started her career at the age of three. All eleven of Temple's first features (beginning with *Stand Up and Cheer*) were introduced to Indianapolis audiences at the Apollo. Another film geared to youngsters was the introduction of Charlotte Henry as Alice for an all-star Paramount production of *Alice in Wonderland,* which lasted only one week. Other more successful films starred Dick Powell and Joan Blondell,

The popular Apollo dismissed all its musicians once it had installed a new sound system and switched to films. Bass Photo Company Collection, Indiana Historical Society.

Deanna Durbin, and Sonja Henie, "queen of the silvery skates." It also offered film versions of novels by a number of Indiana authors. Five of those were by Gene Stratton Porter, four by Booth Tarkington, three by George Ade, and one by Edward Eggleston.

The Apollo's first-run policy was altered in the fall of 1937 when the theater was subleased to the Greater Indianapolis Amusement organization, which now handled bookings at the Indiana and Circle. Successful films at those theaters were moved to the Apollo for additional showings. That lease arrangement ended thirty months later, and the theater never really recovered. After some false starts, it was closed in June 1941.

Over at the Indiana, stage attractions did not end after Davis's second departure. In March 1932, an advertisement announced, "The Indiana scoops the show world for the first time in history." This was the booking of a Broadway musical on a motion picture theater stage. The show (streamlined to ninety minutes) was George Gershwin's *Girl Crazy*, featuring such popular songs as "I Got Rhythm" and "Embraceable You." Also included was a feature film. The highest seat price at the Indiana was 65¢. (Tickets for the Broadway version had sold for $4.40.) No name star was listed in this version of the show, which introduced Ethel Merman and Ginger Rogers to Broadway when it opened in 1930.

Seventeen-year-old Kitty Carlisle had the lead in the musical *Rio Rita*, produced by Florenz Ziegfeld, first seen in 1927. A month later, Broadway's 1919 musical comedy *Irene* was the Indiana attraction, with "Alice Blue Gown" one of its most popular songs.

One week after *Irene* played the Indiana, another highly popular Broadway musical, *Sally*, was booked, again from Ziegfeld. Music was by Jerome Kern. "Look for the Silver Lining" was introduced in this show. *Sally* had opened on Broadway in 1920 with Marilyn Miller as its lead. Twenty-year-old Mary Eaton, groomed by Ziegfeld to be Miller's successor, had the lead at the Indiana.

Another highlight of this era at the Indiana occurred on the screen rather than live. It was fitting that the popular crooner who had appeared numerous times on the theater's stage should be seen locally first on its screen. Dick Powell starred in Warner Brother's *Blessed Event*, the first of his many movie musicals.

One month later, the *Indianapolis Recorder* ran a front-page article claiming that both the Indiana and the Circle were going to close because audiences had been subjected to the release of "nauseating acid." Many, the paper stated, were forced to leave the theater. Both theaters promptly ran advertisements in the *Star*, *News*, and *Times* that this would not happen.

In July 1933, the Circle presented the highly popular all-black show *Shuffle Along* for a week. Management

During this 1930s era, the Indiana highly publicized an "all colored revue" featuring Bill Robinson, "creator of the famous stair-step dance." The show was Hot from Harlem. Reflective of an attitude of the time was an announcement in newspaper advertisements that the show's last performance would be for "colored people only" starting at 10 PM. Indiana University student Amy Wilson referred to what happened that night in her master's thesis. Some 800 African Americans staged a protest outside the theater, challenging such discrimination. Robinson had requested that the theater, which did not allow African Americans to attend, make this performance available to them. He got into a shouting match with two of the protesters, who were arrested and charged with inciting a riot. Charges were later dropped.

143

Facing. Kitty Carlisle in *Rio Rita* in 1927. Vincent Burke Collection.

announced that one performance would be offered at Tomlinson Hall for a black audience. The *Recorder's* response reflected the bitter acceptance of the time:

> The gates of the wall of race prejudice that bar the entrance of colored people to the Circle theater will be flung wide long enough next Wednesday, July 26, to permit the city's biggest offering of the current season to shed its radiant splendor among the colored folk. . . . The show will begin at 10:30 and a dance, music for which will be furnished by the renowned Eubie Blake's orchestra of fourteen pieces, will follow.

Since African Americans were not welcome at many of the mainline downtown theaters, seldom did one find a downtown theater advertisement in the *Recorder*. However, there were exceptions when well-known black performers were involved.

It is doubtful that many of the minority population responded, since the Walker was a far better theater. When Ethel Waters came to English's in *Mamba's Daughters,* the black population in effect was invited through the *Recorder,* and the same invitation was extended by the Murat when it booked a musical pageant of spirituals. Over twenty leading actors were in the cast from the South that came to town for three days, joining 150 members of choirs from local churches.

In 1939 "prominent African Americans" joined what the *Recorder* called a volunteer workers' army of 3,000 persons to take part in a drive for the Indianapolis Community Fund. This took place at the Murat as a kickoff for 400 community campaigns to be held in October. Principal speaker at the rally was Charles Taft, the son of President William Howard Taft. Theater integration was beginning, but it was still a rarity.

By the early '30s, Paramount-Publix had stepped out of management of both the Circle and the Indiana, returning control to the Circle Theater Company. The Indiana continued its stage and movie policy, with Ed Resener and the concert orchestra in the pit. Stage attractions included appearances by vocalist Kate Smith, Fats Waller and his orchestra, a ninety-minute version of *George White's Scandals,* starring young dance sensation Eleanor Powell, and a two-day visit by one of radio's most popular nightly radio programs, *Amos and Andy.*

A signal that all was not financially well at the state's largest theater was the startling announcement that it would be closed for the summer of 1933. One month before it reopened in September, the Circle Theater Company announced it was surrendering control once again. Both the Indiana and Circle would now be run by the Indianapolis Theater Management Associates, Inc. Personnel included Sam Katz, one of the founders of the Balaban-Katz theater chain in Chicago, and Milton Feld, who had been a field supervisor for Paramount-Publix when that organization was in charge of the local houses.

In a story in the *Indianapolis Star* on August 5, a local business executive and member of the Circle Company Board, Leo Rappaport, stated: "We have known these men well and favorably for a great many years as outstanding figures in the field of motion picture entertainment. We have full confidence in their ability to operate these theaters to the satisfaction of the public."

The big theater came back to life with a new vigor when it reopened in September. It announced it was offering "a dazzling revue," devised and staged by its new managing director, Edward Weisfeldt. It featured network radio comics Colonel Stoopnagle and Budd and drummer "extreme" Jack Powell along with Lou Forbes and the "augmented" Indiana concert orchestra with "12 dancing damsels." A lighthearted feature film, *Three-Cornered Moon*, with Claudette Colbert completed the program, which earned favorable newspaper reviews.

The following week's offering at the Indiana stressed its feature film over its stage attraction. The film was a romantic comedy drama, *One Sunday Afternoon*, starring Gary Cooper. Onstage was Bob Hope and a musical comedy revue. Five weeks later, manager Ace Berry chose to book a show that wasn't typical of the place's usual entertainment fare. He brought in a vaudeville show that headlined Sally Rand and her "famous fan dance," which had drawn crowds at the 1933 World's Fair in Chicago.

A few days before her arrival, Miss Rand notified Ace Berry that during her number she wanted the theater orchestra in the pit in front of her rather than onstage behind her. The reason for the request was left to the imagination of the prospective ticket purchaser. The issue was highly publicized, and Berry replied that he would have to think about it.

Attending the first performance were Mrs. B. B. McDonald, president of the Indianapolis Federation of Civic and Community Clubs, and three policewomen. Their assignment was to judge the performance and report their findings to the city's board of safety. A portion

• • • • • • • • • • • • •

Miss Rand got lots of attention from the local papers. A front-page story in the Indianapolis Star showed her at Union Station under the headline "Sally Rand wears clothes after all on arrival here.... as to dance, well!!!" She also was anything but subtle about her arrival. With her were a secretary, a maid, two trunks filled with those famous fans, and twelve other pieces of luggage. With sirens blazing, a sizable motorcycle police escort saw her safely to the stage door.

• • • • • • • • • • • • •

145

In the spring of 1935 the Indiana suddenly announced it was going to host a stage revue that had been on Broadway for a year. I was determined to go. The timing was right. My mother's sister was coming down from Chicago for a week. With her would be my cousin David, three weeks my elder. We were both nine years old. The sisters were always looking for something to keep us busy while they reminisced about their childhood years. I sold them on going to the Indiana. The advertisement said the stage show was the "Casino De Paree Revue with 20 brilliant scenes" that included "32 of the World's Most Alluring Blondes, Brunettes, and Redheads." All I got from that was an exciting show onstage. The sisters didn't really see the ad. After standing in line outside the theater for what seemed to be an interminable time, we were guided to four distant seats in the balcony. Several of the "20 Brilliant Scenes" involved bedrooms with men and women getting in and out of bed. I didn't follow the dialogue too well, but David decided it had to fit that

(continued on facing page)

of Mrs. McDonald's report reads as follows: "Sally Rand as viewed by her audience at her opening performance, produced an artistic effort rather than the bizarre effect of a burlesque show. Her filmy garment might seem insufficient, but her graceful manipulation of her fans concealed her body from view so that the effect produced is beautiful rather than vulgar."

Fifteen consecutive weeks of stage and film attractions at the Indiana ended with the appearance of Howard Thurston, billed now as the "master magician of all times," with new bargain prices offered. All seats were 25¢ until 6 PM and 40¢ thereafter with youngsters ages twelve and under admitted for a dime. A few weeks later, the theater went dark for ten days, announcing it was preparing for the Christmas holiday rush. It reopened Christmas Eve with an all-film policy. On New Year's Eve, Dessa Byrd made one of her final appearances at the Indiana with a "jamboree songfest" along with the Devore Sisters from local radio station WKBF (later WIRE).

The theater that had been the place for popular stage and film attractions from the time it opened now turned to highly popular films from Paramount to keep it going. These included just about all the films starring Fred Astaire and Ginger Rogers, Bing Crosby, Bob Hope, Dick Powell, Claudette Colbert, Irene Dunne, Bette Davis, and Shirley Temple. Dessa Byrd's last appearance at the theater was in November 1934 when the musical comedy film *College Rhythm* was booked. She provided a program featuring Indiana college school songs that fit well with the film.

Stage shows at the Indiana didn't go away entirely, but only eleven were booked the last six years of the decade. They included a traveling company that presented Sigmund Romberg's *The Student Prince* (1934), a second appearance of Kate Smith (1934), Fletcher Henderson and his "famous radio orchestra" (1937), and "Ziegfeld's thrill girl," Gypsy Rose Lee (1938).

The grimmest years for the Indiana were 1936 and 1937, when the theater was dark for over fourteen months. In

June 1937, it carried the once banned film, *Ecstasy*, created in Czechoslovakia in 1933 with a widely publicized scene of teenager Hedy Lamar in a nude swimming sequence. It lasted at the Indiana one week. It was an extreme departure from what usually was shown at the theater. More typical was Walt Disney's first full-length cartoon, the immortal *Snow White and the Seven Dwarfs*. This type of movie improved the box office receipts, but not enough to keep the theater open in the summer. The summer policy continued through 1940.

Effective air-conditioning existed at the Indiana and all the rest of the downtown first-run houses by 1932. However, the number of first-run outlets had dropped to four by that summer (Apollo, Lyric, Loew's, Circle). Fortunately for the customers, neighborhood theaters were adding cooling systems, too. They could do it at less cost with smaller auditoriums. Heat waves were not unusual in the 1930s. In 1936, temperatures exceeded 100 degrees for a week in July (106 degrees on July 15). With such severe weather, theaters gained some needed popularity, no matter what they were showing. They were one of the few places at the time that provided such comfort.

Over fifty deaths in Indianapolis were attributed to the extreme heat. There were close to forty theaters operating in the city that summer, thanks to the wisdom of the neighborhood operators.

Although the Indiana was seldom functioning during the summers, its sister theater, the Circle, remained open year-round with one exception. It was closed three weeks in December 1938, while 2,600 new seats were installed. It continued to attract audiences with Paramount and First National (now merged with Warner Brothers) features, occasional stage attractions, and, for a while, organ presentations.

Some of the features were grim, like *All Quiet on the Western Front* (based on Erich Maria Remarque's book), showing World War I from the point of view of the German soldier. But most were lighthearted, like *42nd Street*, with a cast that included Ruby Keeler and Dick Powell, or *Flying Down to Rio*, with Ginger Rogers and

• • • • • • • • • • • • •

word we only whispered in my neighborhood: dirty. David began poking me and giggling. When the "32 Gorgeous Girls" appeared behind a scrim with lights lowered, they appeared to be wearing little or no clothing. David's punches became less subtle along with the giggles. Mother reacted, trying to distract me, by telling me how scenic all this was and, of course, I agreed, though I must admit I was convinced my cousin had gotten on to something. When the curtain descended and we headed for the exits, no references took place in our foursome, and I wasn't going to initiate any, that's for sure. Years later, I read the review by critic Walter Whitworth in the Indianapolis News. Wrote Walter: "There is a chorus that performs various ensemble routines with considerable dexterity. The revue is attractively staged and lighted. The costumes, what there are of them, are likewise attractive." Obviously, that review as well as the ad had slipped by both of our mothers.

• • • • • • • • • • • • •

Another stage attraction at the Circle in 1939 (by now I was 13) caught my attention. Vincent Lopez with what he called his "suave swing orchestra" was surrounded with other talent. It included Betty Hutton, billed as "America's No. 1 jitterbug," Patricia Ellis, "lovely singing star of the screen," humorist Ben Blue, and the comedy team of Kate Smith's radio show, Abbott and Costello. After two shows, I advanced to the stage door via the alley to get autographs. Miss Ellis obliged. The three comedians were too absorbed in a game of poker to sign anything. I could see them through a low-level window. Two of them were smoking cigars. It was a bit disillusioning.

Fred Astaire making their first of many films together, or the Marx Brothers or Harold Lloyd films that always produced laughter. Two others of note were Claudette Colbert and Clark Gable in the Oscar-winning romantic comedy *It Happened One Night* and Katharine Hepburn in *Little Women*.

Stage offerings varied. The former occupant of the Indiana, Charlie Davis and his Joy Gang, appeared two weeks. The Mills Brothers, radio and recording vocalists, were booked twice, and two popular NBC radio personalities who posed as colorful rural characters, Lum and Abner, made two visits. There was the "king of the banjo," Eddie Peabody, with "a host of stars" in the *Happiness Show,* and there was the "star entertainer of the twenties speakeasies," as *The Filmgoer's Companion* described Mary Louise "Texas" Guinan. She headed a show that the Circle management warned was not suitable for children.

Organ presentations were a part of the Circle programs up to late 1932 when the popular Dessa Byrd's long tenure there ended with melodies from the operetta *The Desert Song*. She continued to make appearances at the Indiana for another two years.

The growing popularity of contemporary musicians through radio and records no doubt triggered an interest by the Circle ownership to book orchestras periodically on its stage. It started out with a "Harlem swing" orchestra lead by Don Redman, featuring vocalist Ella Mae Waters. (I stayed through two shows.)

Early in 1938 it broke some attendance records with a "sizzling red hot battle of swing." Not one but two bands were on stage, side by side. One was directed by trumpeter "Sugar Blues" Clyde McCoy, the other, a group that had worked on Jack Benny's radio show, by Don Bestor. I was in the audience and discovered that the ad headline was misleading. In reviewing the show for the *Indianapolis Star,* Corbin Patrick stated, "They're ace bands, each in its way and the audience fortunately isn't asked to choose between them. If we had to decide, we'd say it's a draw." A few weeks later, I was ecstatic when Fred Waring and his Pennsylvanians and his "entire radio show" moved into the Circle, offering five performances a day. I saw this one four times in two visits.

Jimmy Dorsey and his orchestra caught my attention a few weeks later. That's when I fell in love with vocalist Helen O'Connell, who was teamed with Bob Eberle. I was too awed even to try to get autographs.

Downtown theater activity had been reduced in the 1930s, but it was still a center of excitement if one was young and experiencing it all for the first time. Just a few steps away from the Circle was another spot that was establishing records and drawing fans to stage shows. Eventually a great many of the bands that thrived on swing would more than match the Circle at the Lyric.

15

The 1930s and
Its Challenges II

The busiest theater stage in Indianapolis throughout most of the 1930s was at 133–139 N. Illinois Street, the site of the Lyric. Most weeks were filled with vaudeville performers and eventually popular swing bands along with feature films. The performers, possessing a variety of talents, were still provided by the RKO (Radio-Keith-Orpheum) circuit. There was the five-year-old "child wonder" Baby Rose Marie. There was crooning troubadour Nick Lucas. There were those wild Hoosiers, Olsen and Johnson, and there was Blackstone, the "world's master magician," to keep customers coming back for more.

Unfortunately, economic conditions at first limited the crowds, and stage bookings were costly. Visiting performers, house musicians, and backstage personnel all had to be paid. Offering some of the best talent available didn't always guarantee success at the box office. For example, one week a star of the future, Bob Hope, appeared in a routine onstage titled "Keep Smiling," and a few weeks later, a popular movie clown of the previous silent era, Harry Langdon, paid a visit. Response both weeks was modest.

In the summer of 1931, the Lyric tried to improve its film selection by joining the Apollo in an arrangement with Universal. The *Indianapolis Star*'s Corbin Patrick observed that "Universal generally succeeds in landing one or two of its special productions among the box office leaders each season." Fifteen months later, both theaters changed their minds and signed an exclusive deal with RKO Radio pictures.

Apparently still not satisfied with customer response, during the 1932 Christmas holiday the Lyric announced it was bringing in a resident musical company to produce vaudeville programs. This change included a master of ceremonies and a thirty-member chorus line. It was abandoned after eight weeks due to a wage dispute. Lyric management had asked its nineteen union employees to take a salary reduction of 25 percent. The answer was no, and the Lyric announced it was closing indefinitely.

How the wage issue was settled was not reported in the local press, but the Lyric was back in business two months later with what it called "something new in vaudeville revue." A new producer was hired, and the *Indianapolis Star* revealed that "visiting acts will be 'dressed up' with the band on stage and a [new] line of chorus girls doing three or four nifty routines." The theater had a gala reopening with a ninety-minute stage show, headlined by radio comedian Joe Penner. It also provided eleven scenes and costumes for the girls that were shipped all the way from New York City. Once again a new policy ended in eight weeks. This time the Lyric said it was dropping stage shows for the summer and would continue to provide first-run film programs.

New life for the Lyric was just ahead, however. The Fourth Avenue Amusement Company surrendered its sublease with the Washington and Illinois Realty Company of Indianapolis. Owners petitioned that a long lease with W. and I. be dissolved, and it was accomplished through a probate court order.

It is ironic that the first summer the big Indiana was closed (1933) was the same summer the Lyric, now the city's only vaudeville house, would return to the hands of its creator. First of all, his intent was to restore it to its former vaudeville popularity.

Corbin Patrick expressed it well in the *Indianapolis Star:* "We understand on good authority that he [Olson] will reestablish immediately the seven act vaudeville policy under which he operated the popular amusement place successfully." Patrick also hit on a most significant point when he added: "Success at the Lyric in Mr. Olson's fifteen-year regime is generally attributed to the fact that he gave personal attention to the acts that he booked for his stage and was a liberal spender of money in building the shows that he wanted. He is known as a great lover of good vaudeville and it is 'in the air' that he does not intend cutting the corners on acts in favor of feature pictures."

Olson's second Lyric era began on the first day of September 1933 with seven acts of metropolitan vaudeville featuring the Watson Sisters (vocalists) and a film program of short subjects (no feature). Within three weeks there was a disruption. The motion picture machine operators claimed they were entitled to eleven more dollars a week in salary based on a previous agreement that involved their union and the downtown theaters. Olson said, "The [local] theater business can-

153

154

Above. Before the summer of 1933 was over, the Lyric's future brightened. Charles Olson, shown here with theater musician Walt Jackson, came out of retirement to once again run the theater he had built. He could afford the investment. In 1927 he had sold his local theatrical interests for $1.2 million. Photographer Ray Conolly.

Facing. Olson's first season featured big stage productions that were not always geared to family tastes. One week there was *Broadway-Go-Round,* which included the "sensuous, daring dance of life featuring the Golden Girl on the giant revolving stage." Photographer Ray Conolly.

not stand it." He shut down for a month. By Thanksgiving he had restored stage shows. Again, the outcome over wages was not revealed publicly.

Another Olson booking raised some eyebrows as to its acceptability. Just days after bank robber John Dillinger was gunned down by police in Chicago as he exited a southside movie house, his father appeared onstage at the Lyric. It was billed as "Hear kindly father tell about his son's life and his visit home while a whole nation sought him." Accompanying him were a brother and a sister. It was limited to five days and was the only stage offering that summer.

Stage shows returned to the Lyric on August 31, 1934, with a show out of New York City titled *Harlem Rhapsody,* featuring a Dixieland orchestra. Chances are that not even Olson could have predicted the significance of this moment at his theater.

Above. *Harlem Rhapsody* would be the first of 253 consecutive weeks of stage and film shows at the Lyric. If any other theater in the country matched that, no claims were ever made. Photographer Ray Conolly.

Left. Ed Resener, whose musical association with the Circle and Indiana reached back to 1916, was directing the house orchestra during this record-breaking era at the Lyric. Photographer Ray Conolly.

The timing was favorable because the only other theaters offering any stage attraction competition, the Indiana, Circle, and Loew's, offered such entertainment only occasionally.

While the Lyric continued to book rather sophisticated revues from time to time, shows that most parents would not feel were appropriate for their children, most weeks were family friendly, as Olson lived up to expectations and booked strong vaudeville talent. Many of these performers were early in their careers. They included Red Skelton, ventriloquist Edgar Bergen and Charlie McCarthy, Abbott and Costello, the Ritz Brothers, Hugh Herbert, and Imogene Coca. All would become popular on radio, movies, or television.

Vaudeville at the Lyric didn't go away by any means. Frequently vaudevillians were scheduled along with an orchestra to add variety to the show. Photographer Ray Conolly.

I had missed two days of school the week Tommy Dorsey arrived. When I announced Saturday morning that I wanted to head for the Lyric, Mother said no. I argued long enough to frustrate her into saying, "You will have to take this up with your father." I still don't know how I managed it. He took one look at me and muttered, "Oh, let him go." I went, arriving near the start of the first stage show. At the time Dorsey's men were doing a rare soft and quiet number, "All or Nothing at All." The Indianapolis News reviewer noted: "Tommy Dorsey's persuasive syncopations are filling the auditorium of the Lyric this week. The band's major virtues and individual virtuosi are obviously known to the young generation which was out in full force."

The following week I had a perfect seventh-grade attendance record and was cleared for the Benny Goodman adventure the following Saturday. I got there in time to see the first number, the Goodman theme song, "Let's Dance." He then stepped to the mike and uttered two words, "Hold Tight." The band went to town with that one and a whole lot more, like "And the Angels Sing" and "One O'Clock Jump," featuring Goodman and trumpeter Ziggy Elman. There also was "Deep Purple," sung by Martha Tilton, and lively swing numbers featuring Lionel Hampton. The crowd that day was so intense that Goodman and the theater agreed to six shows. I saw the first three. The film portion was limited to the sixty-minute feature, The Secret Service of the Air, starring Ronald Reagan.

Sometimes they were headliners themselves. Red Skelton appeared one week with Roger Pryor and his orchestra. Vocalist Tony Martin did the same with the Anson Weeks orchestra, and two movie stars of the time, Edmund Lowe and Ann Dvorak, were on the bill with Lawrence Welk and his orchestra.

The Lyric became the place to go to see the highly popular orchestra stars whose identity arose thanks to radio and recordings.

Both Dorsey and Goodman did their weekly radio network broadcasts from the stage of the Lyric. Actually, fans had two chances to see these broadcasts because there were repeats for the West Coast.

Two of the most highly regarded swing music orchestras played the Lyric in consecutive weeks in 1939. "That sentimental gentleman of swing," Tommy Dorsey, and his talented group played the first week. Courtesy *Indianapolis Star.*

Herb Sanford, in his book *Tommy and Jimmy: The Dorsey Years,* stated that Hoagy Carmichael's mother, Lida Carmichael, played the "Maple Leaf Rag" on the piano and stole the show from Hoagy and Tommy. That also was the night Dorsey sent out for food for twelve youngsters who had been occupying front row seats since the afternoon.

During the amazing 253-week run of stage presentations, 67 of them featured popular orchestras. The following is a list of musical groups on the Lyric stage from August 1934 to July 1939, when another employee strike occurred. Numbers indicate repeat visits:

Benny Meroff and the NBC Orchestra

Charlie Davis and his Joy Gang

Noble Sissle and his International Orchestra (3)
    with vocalist Lena Horne in 2nd visit

Buddy Rogers and his own California Cavaliers (2)

Barney Rapp and his New Englanders (2)

Duke Ellington, Harlem's Aristocrat of Jazz (2)

Frank and Milt Britton and their band

Bob Crosby and his orchestra (2) with his modern
    Dixieland orchestra, 2nd visit

Horace Heidt and his Alemite Brigadiers (3) with
    comic Art Carney, 2nd visit sets attendance record

Ina Ray Hutton and her Melodears

Fats Waller and his CBS Swing Band (2)

Roger Pryor and his orchestra (2) with "new
    comedy sensation" Red Skelton, 2nd visit

Phil Splitalny and his World Famous All-Girl Band
    (2) featuring Maxine and her haunting voice and
    Evelyn and her magic violin

Ted Lewis with his band and his Rhythm
    Rhapsody Revue (3)

Dave Apollon and his Tropical Swing Band (3)

Cab Calloway and his Cotton Club Orchestra

Eddy Duchin and his piano magic and orchestra
    (3) established a twenty-five-year all-time
    attendance record in their first visit

Mal Hallett and his orchestra

The man voted by musicians to be the world's greatest clarinetist, Benny Goodman, frequently called the "king of swing," and his orchestra played the second week. Courtesy *Indianapolis Star.*

159

Tommy Dorsey's guest on his broadcast over the NBC red network was Hoosier songwriter-pianist-vocalist Hoagy Carmichael. Hoagy's mother, Lida, who lived in Indianapolis, also appeared. Photographer Ray Conolly.

Little Jack Little, his orchestra, and his own revue

Eddie Mallory and his famous swing band

Ted Weems with vocalist Perry Como and whistling star Elmo Tanner (2)

Louis Armstrong, the "Trumpet King of Swing," and orchestra

Wayne King, his famous orchestra and Grand Revue (2)

Henry Busse, "the trumpet king," and his famous orchestra (2)

Swing and Sway with Sammy Kaye and his orchestra

Happy Felton and orchestra (2)

Phil Harris, star of *The Jell-O Program Starring Jack Benny,* and his
   orchestra (set box office record)

Ted Fio Rito and his famous orchestra

Benny Goodman's shows were broadcast by CBS. He is shown onstage doing a number with his popular sextet. Due to a heavy crowd,
he agreed to do six shows on Saturday. Photographer Ray Conolly.

Jan Garber and his orchestra

Gene Krupa and his own Famous Swing Orchestra

Ozzie Nelson, his orchestra, and vocalist Harriet Hilliard (2)

Baseball's Pepper Martin and his Mudcat Band

George Olsen and his Music of Tomorrow orchestra

Glen Gray and the Casa Loma Orchestra

Herbie Kay and his orchestra

Hal Kemp and his orchestra

"Genial musical star" Frankie Masters and his orchestra

Tommy Dorsey, That Sentimental Gentleman of Swing, and orchestra with
   vocalists Edythe Wright and romantic baritone Jack Leonard

Benny Goodman, America's Favorite Swingmaster, with Camel Caravan's
   "swing school" stars Martha Tilton, Lionel Hampton, and Ziggy Elman
Anson Weeks and his famous orchestra with vocalist Tony Martin
Orrin Tucker and orchestra with Sweet Singer Bonnie Baker
Jay Mills and Dean Hudson orchestras in a Battle of Music
Abe Lyman and his orchestra and his California Revue with local
   vocalist Frankie Parrish
Joe Sanders and his orchestra
Gray Gordon and his Tic Toc Rhythm Orchestra
Clyde McCoy and his Sugar Blues Orchestra
Johnny "Scat" Davis and his orchestra

At the time, the Lyric had fifty-two employees, including eight stagehands who were union members. The eight wanted a $5 a week raise, which would have put them at $60.50 a week. Olson wouldn't budge, and the theater went dark for eleven weeks.

Perhaps Olson's associate and manager of the theater, Ted Nicholas, was a little more patient than his boss. He had been described more than once by the local media as personable and likeable. At any rate, salary increases were granted not only to the stagehands but also to film projectionists and musicians. Individual increases were not revealed, but the *Indianapolis Star* stated that the total wage increases came to $2,000 a week.

The reopening attraction at the Lyric (September 22, 1939) was Ben Bernie and his orchestra (Bernie called them his "lads") with vaudeville entertainers and a typical lighthearted movie titled *The Cowboy Quarterback*. Fan response was impressive. The show broke a one-day record for attendance. Another consecutive stage show string was under way, with nearly half the bookings being orchestra concerts.

Many of the same popular orchestras returned after the theater respite, some with new vocalists. Bob Crosby's Dixieland group now had Doris Day, Benny Goodman had Helen Forrest, Hal Kemp featured Janet Blair, and Tommy Dorsey showed up with Frank Sinatra. (I was in the audience and was not particularly impressed. I couldn't imagine why all the young females squealed every time he started singing.) Herb Sanford noted that Sinatra was making his very first appearance with Dorsey that week of February 2, 1940. Other highly regarded orchestras who appeared were led by Jack Teagarden, Paul Whiteman, Red Nichols, Raymond Scott, John Kirby (with vocalist Maxine Sullivan), and Joe Venuti (with the Andrews Sisters).

The Lyric's onetime prime competitor in vaudeville, the Keith's, continued to struggle into the mid-1930s. Ironically, the Lyric's Olson leased the facility for a week to play a highly publicized Warner Brothers film of Shakespeare's *A Mid-*

summer Night's Dream in 1936. Among its well-known cast members were James Cagney, Olivia de Havilland, Joe E. Brown, Dick Powell, and Mickey Rooney. All seats were reserved with prices ranging from 55¢ to $1.10. Showings were limited to two a day. There is no indication whether or not the booking was highly successful in this city.

Keith's availability in 1933 brought in the Federal Players as an occupant for fifteen months. Dr. Lee Norvelle, head of the drama department at Indiana University, was named head of the Indiana segment of the Federal Works Project (also known as the WPA), established to provide employment during the Great Depression. Seventy-seven people with theatrical experience were hired. Most had formerly been on federal relief. Its director was Charles Berkell, whose stock company had played more than one Indianapolis theater in the past, including Keith's.

Berkell's plays frequently ran for two weeks with humorous themes dominant. Booth Tarkington's *Clarence* was the opener with the top ticket price at 40¢. Customer response was quite successful with two plays achieving attendance records. The biggest hit was Edward Eggleston's *Hoosier Schoolmaster,* and the runner-up was a play written by the theater's manager, Henry K. Burton, *Do unto Others.*

All was going well until the summer of 1937, when the federal government ordered all such theater groups to reduce personnel by 30 percent. An article in the *Indianapolis Star* (June 24, 1937) stated that "the company could not operate efficiently with the reduced basis." During its tenure, 150,000 customers had attended shows at the old theater.

Keith's made a bid in the fall of 1937 to resume its old policy of vaudeville onstage with film features (not always first-run). Prices never got higher than 25¢. Although the management made a mighty try based on newspaper advertisements, the management changed within sixteen months when the lessee, Central City, hired Carl Niesse to be general manager. Niesse initiated double features during the week with vaudeville on weekends, but this idea was short-lived. The theater finished the decade closed more than it was open. There was one very significant evening at Keith's. Indianapolis native Todd Duncan, who was the original Porgy in Broadway's *Porgy and Bess,* appeared there in concert, responding to a request to do so by the YMCA.

While Keith's struggled, the Lyric had found fortune in the arrival of the big band era. Five other downtown houses (Indiana, Circle, Loew's, Apollo, and Walker) turned to sound films for survival. Two more found they could manage by offering burlesque (Colonial and Mutual). English's bookings dropped in number, but it continued offering Broadway theater, and the Murat specialized in classical and semiclassical music that included concerts by the newly formed Indianapolis Symphony Orchestra.

163

16

The Rest of the
1930s Survivors

Facing. The Colonial (later the Fox, 240 N. Illinois Street) was the most fearless, shifting to burlesque from first-run films just when the early talkies were attracting big audiences. Bass Photo Company Collection, Indiana Historical Society.

A nationwide depression failed to chase burlesque theater away from downtown Indianapolis. When the decade began, three houses were offering burlesque shows. The Mutual had been providing them ever since it opened as the Majestic (130 S. Illinois Street) in 1907. The Rialto (17 Kentucky Avenue) had been providing such entertainment off and on since opening as the Family in 1908. The Colonial (later the Fox) theater was more coy about its offerings. Its newspaper advertisements didn't use the term *burlesque* until the 1930s.

The theater booked some of the leading strippers of the day. Enough customers attended to make it the prime burlesque theater in the city with a life that continued until 1961. The Rialto had disappeared by the mid-1930s. The Mutual lowered its curtain permanently in the early 1950s.

During the Colonial's long existence there is no evidence that any of its stage offerings were ever reviewed by any of the city's daily newspapers. There were moments, however, when a burlesque house did make newspaper headlines. In July 1930 the *Indianapolis Star* reported that a local courtroom drew a maximum crowd when Miss Mildred Wood appeared before Municipal Court Judge Clifton Cameron. She had been arrested for "shedding too many clothes at a downtown theater" (the theater was not identified). Reportedly, she had offered to defend herself in court by wearing the attire under question. Judge Cameron promptly declared a delay in the proceedings before Miss Wood had a chance to disrobe. The *Star* article observed that "several rows of seats were emptied promptly as

their occupants began to file toward the door. The judge raised his voice: 'And don't come back. You won't see anything when you do.'" Two days later when it was determined the defendant "bared the upper part of her body" during the show, the judge decided that wasn't offensive and freed her.

There was still no subtlety when it came to burlesque newspaper advertisements. For example, for a week in 1933 the Colonial (Fox) was hosting "a chorus of 20 beautifully, dainty, daring, dashing little devils." Another week the featured performer was Little Egypt, "hotter than the desert sands," and still another, "Paula Lewis outstrips them all."

167

These advertisements brought in customers, but they also continued to spark challenges periodically. In February 1934, Mayor Reginald Sullivan, after meeting with the manager, announced that nudity would be reduced to a minimum in future burlesque presentations. The manager was quoted in the *Star* as saying that the "girls will wear something to speak of in order to comply with a proposed new law."

• • • • • • • • • • • •

The very month that the Hays Code went into effect, the Bandbox (119 N. Illinois Street) booked a film titled White Cargo. Theater advertisements proclaimed that it had been "banned by Will Hays but acclaimed by press and the public [and was] a drama of hot climes, hot tempers, hot romance." It had been produced in England.

• • • • • • • • • • • •

Just how long the new modesty measure was honored is questionable. In less than a year, the Colonial was promoting what it called "a mammoth stage show" starring "Olympia, daughter of the gods and her nudists," along with "a host of California's sun-tanned beauties."

Early in this decade the film industry, determined to head off growing criticism for offering "immoral material," adopted a code to assure the public of its wholesome intentions. It was felt that sound effects had taken films to a new level of reality and that some new prohibitions were necessary. Heading this new policy of "self-discipline" was Will H. Hays, who was in his ninth year as president of the Motion Picture Producers and Distributors of America. The attorney and former U.S. postmaster general was born in Sullivan, Indiana.

What would become known as the Hays Code would, according to local newspapers, "affect directly the character of pictures shown in 22,000 theaters in the country which have an estimated audience of more than two hundred and fifty million persons served weekly by the companies which have given approval to the document." A long list of restrictions included "scenes of passion shall not be introduced when not essential to the plot . . . obscenity in word, gesture, reference, song, joke, or by suggestion is forbidden . . . dances which emphasize indecent movements are to be regarded as obscene . . . indecent or undue exposure is forbidden."

This new policy presumably was followed by the mainline theaters, but the Colonial when it offered films didn't seem to be affected, or at least its ads claimed otherwise. It was quite willing to include warnings in its ads. One week the theater asked, "Is a doctor's consulting room as sacred as a priest's confessional? See the nakedness of life in unclothed despair (adults only)." Another film offering was titled *Sex Madness*, asking the question, "Is your daughter safe? A film that tells all." Close to Christmas 1933, the theater continued to ignore restrictions, offering *This Nude World* with "authentic pictures of nudists."

168

The sizable growth in numbers of theaters throughout the city during the century's first three decades slowed almost to a stop in the 1930s. Only six new theaters opened, compared with twenty-six during the 1920s. Among the new six would be the Vogue (6257 N. College Avenue) built by Carl Niesse.

Several of the larger neighborhood houses offered stage attractions along with second-run films during the early '30s. These theaters included the Fountain Square, where Dessa Byrd's sister, Virginia, became the theater's organist, and

Broad Ripple residents protested when they learned in 1938 that a brand-new theater, the Vogue, was to be constructed nearby. There was fear that it would not succeed and would be replaced by an undesirable occupant. It was a prominent neighborhood theater for many years. Bass Photo Company Collection, Indiana Historical Society.

the Zaring, where future Marion County prosecutor Noble Pearcy appeared as a star in Louise Powell's *Kiddie Revue*. Pearcy was listed as "Indiana's most popular child entertainer." The Rivoli was booking weekend stage shows into 1936.

Two other theaters downtown continued to provide alternatives to Hollywood offerings, although the Depression affected their choice of bookings. Their level of entertainment was more expensive than what was offered at the other downtown facilities, and admission cost considerably more. These theaters, of course, were the Murat and English's.

Although the Mystic Shrine closed the Murat (limiting it to membership use) when the Shubert organization did not renew its lease in 1929, there were those

169

English's opened its 1930-31 season with musical comedy star Fred Stone in Ripples, which also included his daughters, Dorothy and Paula. I was in the audience (at the age of five) for my first look at a Broadway musical. The reason: my father was a big Fred Stone fan. Two moments I remember. Dad alerted me to the fact that Stone always made an unusual entrance. In this show he was supposed to have been kicked out of a barn by a mule. Actually, I learned later, he swung out from a horizontal bar, turned a back somersault, landed on his feet in a tulip bed, and came up smelling a tulip. At another point in the show, he did a fancy dance with crutches. Dad explained that all this was quite remarkable, because three years previously Stone had been told by his doctors that he was through as an actor and acrobat. That prediction

(continued on facing page)

in the fraternal organization who were convinced that there still was a bright future. Considerable money was spent to recondition the structure. The *Star* (September 11, 1931) stated that "the stage has been newly equipped, making it one of the most modern and complete in the country. New seats have been installed, new carpets provided, and the tapestries restored."

The upgrading of the Murat got the attention of two gentlemen who were familiar with the theater scene in Indianapolis. Both Roltare Eggleston and Horace Mitchell had been stage performers in their younger years. Later, Eggleston had served as manager of both the Keith's and English theaters. Mitchell had worked with the Scottish Rite in Indianapolis and had also managed dramatic and musical presentations for the organization. They took over the lease and initiated efforts to resume public entertainment.

Finding performers for the Murat stage was not an easy task in 1931. Over the next twenty-seven months only three bookings were scheduled. The Princeton University Triangle Club, founded by Booth Tarkington, presented one performance of *Spanish Blades* with a cast of forty-five students (December 29, 1931). "A timely lecture" by a member of the British Parliament, Winston Churchill, occurred on February 27, 1932, and an Indianapolis Matinee Musical Chorale concert took place there the same year in May.

The dilemma eased up considerably when the founder and conductor of the newly formed Indianapolis Symphony Orchestra, Ferdinand Schaefer, brought his musicians to the theater in May 1933. It was the orchestra's final concert of its third season, and it was offered free to the public. The orchestra's previous home had been Caleb Mills Hall at Shortridge High School. Its new home would serve the orchestra for the next thirty years.

Bringing the city's symphony orchestra to the Murat was beneficial to both the orchestra and the theater. The orchestra needed a larger facility for both its musicians and its growing audience. The theater badly needed a strong attraction to bring back customers. There also was prestige connected to this decision, which was important to the Mystic Shrine members.

By 1937 a new conductor, Fabien Sevitzky, would head the Indianapolis Symphony Orchestra, and a popular concert series was added to the classical series. This broadened the audience and enhanced the orchestra's image. Some of the soloists who were there in the 1930s included vocalists Lawrence Tibbett, John Charles Thomas, Lauritz Melchior, and Ezio Pinza, and violinists Mischa Elman and Jascha Heifetz. For those who preferred pop music there was the appearance of Phil Splitalney and his Hour of Charm Orchestra, originating its NBC radio program from the theater.

The only time the Murat had a Broadway show on its boards in the 1930s was when a fire at English's made it necessary. In mid-January 1935, *Earl Carroll's Vanities* opened a three-day engagement at English's with a company of one hundred, including comic Ken Murray and "Chaz Chase and the most beautiful girls in the world." Fire broke out at midnight in the theater when it was unoccupied. Scenery and properties were destroyed at an estimated cost of $58,000. The theater's structural damage was limited to $3,000. The second day's performance was canceled. The third day's show moved to the Murat.

The fire moved another Broadway show into the Murat the following week. Dorothy Stone and Ethel Waters headed a cast in a "Music Box sensation," *As Thousands Cheer.*

For well over thirty years, the Valentine Company had managed the English theater, most of those years under the leadership of Ad Miller. During the latter part of that era, the prestigious Circle Theater Company took over the ownership and in 1930 was responsible for extensive improvements. The *Indianapolis Star*'s Robert Tucker wrote on October 19 that "when English's is reopened it will amount practically to a new theater in which attention has been paid to the comfort of patrons and a decorative scheme created which we are assured will be pleasing." By 1931 the theater's manager was Vincent Burke, who started working there in 1897 as an usher. By now the ownership had been renamed the English Theater Company. Burke would be in charge for the rest of the theater's existence. These changes also settled which theater, English's or the Murat, would serve the city as the outlet for Broadway productions.

• • • • • • • • • • • • •

followed injuries he received piloting a small plane. He lost control while attempting a forced landing. In a book Stone authored, Rolling Stone, he wrote: "They put me in a cast from my ankles to my chin and told me that, while I might possibly walk someday, I would never dance again." Indianapolis Star critic Robert Tucker wrote that he had predicted that Stone "would give the new season here a flying start and it so happened." The Oxford Companion to American Theatre states that Stone's shows (including six with his late partner, Dave Montgomery) were all huge hits with the exception of the last two, Ripples and Smiling Faces, the latter playing at English's in March 1932. I saw both, and at ages five and seven, I thought they were wonderful.

• • • • • • • • • • • • •

Operating a legitimate theater in a midwestern city continued to be a challenge in the early 1930s. Costs were considerably more than they were for the movie houses. Musicals were costlier than comedies and dramas with their smaller casts. For example, when the Marx Brothers moved in for a week with their musical, *Animal Crackers,* top price was $4.40 a seat, and the cast numbered 125. That same week one could see feature films at the Apollo, Loew's Palace, or the Circle (a musical romance with Metropolitan Opera star Lawrence Tibbett) at a top price well under 50¢.

Sometimes shows would find a better deal and cancel. This happened to English's twice during the 1930–31 season. Grace George was scheduled to appear in *The First Mrs. Frazier* in April. Robert Tucker called it "one of the smartest and most successful [plays] of the last two years." The theater was notified just three weeks before opening night that the show was bypassing Indianapolis for Chicago. A similar sequence occurred for a scheduled new comedy, *The Old Rascal,* starring the then popular William Hodge. The switch this time involved Fort Wayne, Indiana.

While English's total show bookings were down (258 in the 1920s compared to 136 in the '30s), there was some favorable entertainment offered. One of the most (locally) highly acclaimed musicals was booked for only three performances. It was an all-black cast in *Rhapsody in Black,* starring Ethel Waters. A capacity crowd filled the theater when George Gershwin appeared for one night many months after the Gershwin brothers' Pulitzer Prize winner, *Of Thee I Sing,* played English's.

Cole Porter music was provided twice in shows at English's with *You Never Know,* starring Indianapolis-born Clifton Webb on a tour that was heading for Broadway, and *Leave It to Me,* which already had been there. Three of four Broadway cast members appeared in Indianapolis in the latter show performed on English's stage here in 1939: Sophie Tucker, Victor Moore, and William Gaxton. However, Mary Martin, who struck it big with her rendition of "My Heart Belongs to Daddy," was booked elsewhere.

A number of revues continued to play English's. The most frequent visitor was *Earl Carroll's Vanities.* Its advertisements claimed "sixty scenes of lavish splendor." In 1932 its cast included Jack Benny, two years before he became a Sunday night radio comic icon on NBC. Four editions of the *Vanities* were scheduled in the '30s, but only three of them appeared. That old nemesis, cancellation, struck again. That show appeared in Fort Wayne, presumably because the cast got a cheaper train rate getting back to New York City from that northern Indiana theater.

Some of the more popular comedies included three George Abbott productions: *Three Men on a Horse* with Sheldon Leonard (twice); *Brother Rat,* starring Eddie Bracken (twice); and *Boy Meets Girl,* a show that spoofed Hollywood writers. *Ah Wilderness* starred George M. Cohan, and there was an engagement of George S. Kaufman and Moss Hart's *You Can't Take It with You* prior to its opening in Chicago. Kaufman was here for rehearsals. It previously had opened in New York, where it had won a Pulitzer Prize. In fact, all of the aforementioned productions appeared in Indianapolis within a year after Broadway openings.

Dramas at English's, however, continued to be the most frequent in the 1930s. Ironically, that list was topped by *Tobacco Road. The Oxford Companion to American Theatre* calls this the story of "a shabby, worthless family of sharecroppers who have lost the land their ancestors had long farmed." It was depressing and was panned by most critics. It made four visits to English's in the 1930s and six more in the 1940s. Each and every time it declared it was a farewell tour. That didn't actually happen until John Barton, who played the leading role of Jeeter over 2,000 times, died in 1946.

Some of the finest actors and actresses in legitimate theater at the time performed at English's. Walter Hampden was winding up a long career with seven appearances during this decade, mostly in Shakespearian roles but including a nineteenth-century classic, *Cyrano de Bergerac.* Six visits by Katharine Cornell brought English's audiences a production of *The Taming of the Shrew,* with Maurice Evans and Tyrone Power, and *No Time for Comedy,* one of her most successful plays on Broadway.

Other visitors of note included Walter Huston in *Dodsworth* and Helen Hayes in *Mary of Scotland* and *Victoria Regina.* Husband and wife Alfred Lunt and Lynn Fontanne appeared together in four shows, including *Idiot's Delight,* and a newcomer, Katharine Hepburn, received rave local reviews as the lead player in *Jane Eyre.*

Although the Murat became the home of the Indianapolis Symphony and hosted a number of visiting classical and semiclassical musical bookings, English's went after that audience, too. Symphony orchestras from three cities staged concerts. Those orchestras were from

● ● ● ● ● ● ● ● ● ● ● ● ●

English's made the list of pre-Broadway appearances for No Time for Comedy. It was billed here as a "world premiere." Miss Cornell was appearing in a less serious role, for her, as Linda Paige, an actress who is starring in a series of frivolous comedies authored by her husband, Gaylord Esterbrook, played by Laurence Olivier. She is infuriated when she learns that another woman has convinced him he should turn to more serious dramatic works. The show opened here on March 30, 1939, for 4 performances. It opened on Broadway eighteen days later where it thrived for 185 performances.

● ● ● ● ● ● ● ● ● ● ● ● ●

Cincinnati, St. Louis, and Minneapolis. Violinists Jascha Heifetz, Fritz Kreisler, and Mischa Elman appeared along with pianists Sergei Rachmaninoff and José Iturbi. But the biggest bookings involved vocalists. The list is long and impressive. Marian Anderson, Lily Pons, and Rosa Ponselle were among the women, but the males dominated the numbers. They include John Charles Thomas, Nino Martini, Richard Crooks, Lawrence Tibbett, Nelson Eddy, and six visits by the Don Cossacks Chorus from Russia.

English's during the 1930s did not operate in the summers, except during the summer of 1931, when it offered a twenty-four-week season of plays by the Casey Players, whose leading player was Donald Woods, who would later become successful in Hollywood. Overall, the theater had survived well under the management of Vincent Burke. It is unlikely that anyone at the time would have predicted that within a little over eight years the theater would be gone.

Facing. Ethel Barrymore came to Indianapolis in four Broadway plays, including *The Constant Wife* and *The Kingdom of God*. Vincent Burke Collection.

17

The 1940s, a Decade of
Success and Sadness

F irst-run movies dominated downtown theaters in the 1940s as the city found itself rid of a depression and entertaining larger audiences, many of them affected by a war. Some of them were in uniform, stationed at Fort Harrison or Camp Atterbury, others were saying good-bye to husbands, sons, or daughters, and still others were turning to jobs needed to produce military supplies.

Loew's launched the new decade's movie era in January, nearly two years before Pearl Harbor, with the long-awaited and highly publicized *Gone with the Wind*. It had its gala premiere at 8 PM on a Friday. Night showings and Sunday matinees required reserve seating at $1.10 a ticket. Weekday matinees offered general seating for just 75¢. Business was so successful that the film occupied the theater for four weeks. One year later it returned and stayed for two weeks at lower prices.

Another historic movie introduced to the city at Loew's was Charlie Chaplin's *The Great Dictator*, which was noted for three significant reasons. It made fun of Germany's Nazi leader, it was available to the public thirteen months before we were at war with Germany, and it allowed audiences to hear Chaplin's voice for the first time.

On another level of entertainment, this was the theater that introduced Jane Russell to Indianapolis following a delay of three years due to censorship problems. Produced by Howard Hughes, *The Outlaw* benefited from the delay. *The Filmgoer's Companion* noted that "the publicity campaign emphasized the star's physical attributes." Local audiences responded accordingly. The film stayed at Loew's three weeks.

Most of the bookings, usually double features, tended to be family oriented, however. Hoosier Red Skelton appeared in fourteen films, equaling the number of times a film series on the comic strip *Blondie* with Penny Singleton and Arthur Lake was shown. The list of other MGM, United Artists, and Columbia stars that occupied the screen at the theater would fill a book, starting with the Andy Hardy adventures, the Marx Brothers, Spencer Tracy and Katharine Hepburn, and many, many musicals starring Judy Garland, Gene Kelly, and Mickey Rooney.

Another powerhouse cinema was the Indiana, which had set aside its stage policy. It got the pick of films coming out of Paramount, Universal, 20th Century Fox, and RKO Radio. Rarely did they remain at the theater more than a week. Shows that were held over were sent to the Circle and the Lyric. After the Lyric was sold, its new owner leased it to the Greater Indianapolis Amusement Company, joining the Indiana and the Circle. By 1947 Keith's was leased to the same company.

An indication that the Indiana was doing well was a decision to keep it open year-round. The last time it closed its doors was the summer of 1941. Among its many attractions was Orson Welles's *Citizen Kane,* which the *Filmgoer's Companion* identifies as a production "often acclaimed the best film of all time." Others first seen at the theater were Bing Crosby's *Holiday Inn* and *Going My Way,* Crosby's "Road to . . ." pictures with Bob Hope, *Casablanca, Yankee Doodle Dandy, Pride of the Yankees,* and *It's a Wonderful Life.*

Twice the Indiana was the setting for World War II military emergency assistance for the wounded. When *This Is the Army,* the film version of what originally was an all-military stage revue, came to the Indiana, special plans were made for its premiere. The sponsor was the 11th District American Legion with Governor Henry Schricker and Mayor Robert Tyndall as co-chairmen. All seating was reserved with a top ticket price of $11. Regular prices were restored during an unprecedented three-week stay. Seventy-five thousand was the customer count for the first week.

Six months later, the General Hospital Band from Fort Harrison performed on the Indiana stage for another military fund-raiser. Sponsored by all of the Indianapolis theaters, it netted over $400,000.

This was the same year (1942) that Indianapolis had responded to what the *Indianapolis Star* called the first state war bond rally (January) held in the United States since the war began. The newspaper's owner, Eugene C. Pulliam, was the executive chairman of the defense savings staff.

Fort Wayne–born actress Carole Lombard came back to help inaugurate the campaign at the Cadle Tabernacle and the statehouse. The one-day sale totaled over $2 million. Anxious to return to her husband, Clark Gable, in Hollywood, she decided not to travel by train but managed to get on a military flight at the last minute. The plane crashed into a mountain in Nevada, killing Lombard, her mother, and nineteen others aboard the plane.

Hollywood actress Carole Lombard came to Indianapolis to
sell war bonds at the Cadle Tabernacle and the statehouse
on January 16, 1942. Courtesy *Indianapolis Star.*

Six months later, a colorful, energetic bandleader named Kay Kyser and his musicians came to Indianapolis for a week's engagement at the Circle. He was well known due to a weekly broadcast on CBS radio. He showed up a day early so he could stage another war bond rally, this one on the south side of Monument Circle. He raised pledges of $212,000, and the following Monday he raised more pledges, once again on Monument Circle.

Kyser also set new records at the Circle, offering five performances a day. Not bad for a leader who was making his first theater appearance, but he also had talented performers that included vocalist Mike Douglas, who a few years later would become a successful TV talk show host. When Kyser departed after a one-week visit, he had performed before nearly 80,000 people, close to 20 percent of the city's population.

Kyser had no doubt convinced the theater that it had made the right move in resuming stage shows, primarily orchestras. They would not appear every week because they would not always be available. Negotiations were under way with Glenn Miller and Clyde McCoy, whose orchestras were quite popular, when both ended up in military uniforms. Hoosier Claude Thornhill brought his orchestra to the Circle, just days before he was to report for naval duty. A few months later, the theater's manager, Arthur Baker, departed for army duty.

Just about every popular orchestra in the United States, known thanks to radio, records, and previous appearances at the Lyric, now visited the Circle. The most frequent visitor was Sammy Kaye and his orchestra, with his "So you want to lead a band?" contest that involved members of the audience. The shows still were accompanied by what might be called vaudeville acts to broaden the entertainment.

With the Lyric stage silent, the theater for the most part was used for additional showings of films. However, just a few months before the decade came to an end, the theater announced it was going to revive stage entertainment. It started with Roy Acuff and his Grand Ole Opry show. Others to follow were Tex Ritter, *Ted Mack & the*

Many years ago, when I was writing a series of stories for a local magazine, I did one on Kyser, who was living in Boston. He had given up show business and become manager of films and broadcasting for the First Church of Christ, Scientist. He refused to be interviewed but sent me a note: "I remember well our week at the Circle in 1942. We stayed at a hotel that backed up to the theater (Washington Hotel), and I recall going out the stage door and quickly entering the back of the hotel."

Original Amateur Hour, and what the theater called "big-time vaudeville" with Art Mooney and his orchestra. All this was tentative. The Lyric's future would be on its screen.

Keith's continued to struggle. In May 1941, the Burton-Daggett Stock Company occupied the theater for a few weeks. A member of the company was local actress Elizabeth Kirk. She recalls that the Indianapolis newspapers came up with favorable reviews, but the summer heat was a key problem, since the theater did not have air-conditioning. Casts rehearsed at the Indianapolis Athletic Club.

The theater came back to life nine months later when a group of Chicago showmen would not only operate the facility but would bring vaudeville back with an orchestra headed by Ed Resener. Shows would run Thursday through Sunday with film features included. Maximum ticket price was 44¢. The timing was good. The *Indianapolis Star* had reported that many had been outraged because the city had had no vaudeville after the Lyric's policy changed. By mid-April 1944 the *Star* reported that vaudeville success continued at a time when many showmen were convinced it was dead. Keith's also proudly reminded the city that it was the only theater in the Midwest manned by an all-girl staff.

Stage headliners who made frequent visits during a time when military personnel were always looking for entertainment included Blackstone the magician, singer Frank Parrish, emcee Cliff "Ukulele Ike" Edwards, Buster West and Lucille Page, a young George Goebel, and Private First Class Donald O'Connor in a "Hollywood revue." By 1946, with the war over, the stage era shut down, and Keith's switched back to double features.

The Fox reinstalled a burlesque policy that became dominant for that type of entertainment in the city. Closed for two years, it reopened in the fall of 1940. The Walker continued with film features, though seldom were they first-run attractions. Those were shown to the white-only audiences downtown. That policy continued in residential neighborhoods. In *Irvington Stories,* Larry Muncie noted that the manager of the Sheridan, which was located near homes occupied by blacks, unsuccessfully attempted to admit them. The manager was fired for his effort.

Discrimination at three southside movie theaters ended when officials of the NAACP and the Community Relations Council represented a black couple who were not allowed seats at the Sanders, the Fountain Square, or the Granada. Down at the southern Indiana mining town of Princeton, a theater was allowing black customers just three days a week and was barring them from using the restrooms. The policy change was credited to the work of Indianapolis attorney Henry Richardson Jr. Over to the east in Richmond, two women were told they must sit in the balcony at the Tivoli. A Wayne County circuit court judge ruled that this was a violation of the Indiana Civil Rights Law. Similar incidents in the

By the 1940s, as an Irvington (eastside) teenager, I attended the Irving Theater on weekends, sometimes with a date. The challenge was to pick just the right moment to put one's arm around the adjacent seat where the date was sitting. I chose to pick the moment when the screen story became humorous. It usually worked. Bass Photo Company Collection, Indiana Historical Society.

mainline theaters in downtown Indianapolis either did not happen or were not reported. By the 1950s, however, most of the theaters were running advertisements in the *Recorder*.

Small downtown theaters in Indianapolis that had once filled the area began dropping out in the 1930s. By the 1940s there were only a few left. One of them was the Cozy, 136 N. Illinois Street, which was specializing in "adult-only" films. Others were the Ambassador, Alamo, and Rodeo. Small theater success was found elsewhere, on the fringe areas of downtown and in neighborhoods throughout the city. For the most part they offered films that had already been shown downtown, but many of their patrons could walk to their box offices. They were convenient. Their number reached nearly forty by the early 1940s.

One key indication that the neighborhood theater business was economically attractive was a decision by Charles Olson, who had been so successful at the downtown Lyric. He purchased five theaters and became reaffiliated with the Lyric and a brand-new neighborhood house, the Vogue at 63rd Street and College Avenue.

Local theater veteran Joseph Cantor acquired five more picture houses, as they were called, including a newly built theater that would be the Esquire at 30th and North Illinois Street. This is where many foreign films were first seen in the Indianapolis area. These films came primarily from Italy, France, and England. When Noël Coward's *Blithe Spirit* was shown, parents were warned not to bring their children. The Esquire also was the first to bring back some comedy classics featuring W. C. Fields and Harold Lloyd.

Other neighborhood developments were involved in what was claimed to be the city's first deluxe neighborhood house, the Zaring. It enlarged its seat capacity to well over 1,000. The revitalized Cinema on East 16th Street managed to obtain an exclusive engagement of Laurence Olivier's film *Henry V,* and the Coronet at Talbot and 22nd Street handled an exclusive showing of the British production of *The Red Shoes* for three weeks.

All this was an indication that downtown theaters had some more competition. Drive-ins also were beginning to appear. Midwest Drive-in Theaters, Inc., purchased a seventy-acre site northeast of Indianapolis and introduced the city to its first one. It opened in June 1940 at 9300 Pendleton Pike.

Two other houses downtown continued to provide customers with legitimate theater, as it was called, live and onstage. The Murat and English's still offered varied entertainment.

While just about every classical musical celebrity of the time visited the Murat, it continued to offer extensive pop music specialists, too. Among them were orchestras headed by Sammy Kaye, Eddie "Jazz" Condon, Duke Ellington, Woody Herman, Spike Jones, Louis Armstrong, and Stan Kenton. There was the unexpected: Don McNeil and the Breakfast Club radio broadcast from its stage, the Shrine Circus, a "spicy, daring" presentation of *Maid in the Ozarks*, and eight acts of "good old vaudeville" with forty performers and a large orchestra.

It was the home base for the Indianapolis Symphony Orchestra, but that didn't mean it would always be conventional. While it featured such soloists as Ezio Pinza, Richard Crooks, Fritz Kreisler, and Jascha Heifetz, it also could lighten up during its local pop concerts. Guests included Oscar Levant, Fred Waring, and Tommy Dorsey. Waring and Dorsey even shared the podium with the Indianapolis Symphony's conductor, Fabien Sevitzky.

Music also could be found at English's, of course, but it usually was part of a Broadway musical. Rodgers and Hammerstein's *Oklahoma,* which set new standards in integrating song and story, played to sellout crowds twice in Indianapolis during two one-week visits.

Cole Porter's music was heard the week that *Du Barry Was a Lady* paid a visit. Advertisements called it the "best girl show of the year" with "50 sylphlike ladies in waiting." Porter's contribution included "Do I Love You?" and "Friendship." Peru, Indiana, where Porter was born, also provided the world of show business with John "Ole" Olsen. He and his partner, Harold Johnson, who were professionally known as Olsen and Johnson, visited the theater twice with their madcap review called *Hellzapoppin'.* When it closed in New York, it had the distinction of being the longest running musical (at the time) ever to play on Broadway. Another one of their shows appearing at English's was *Sons of Fun,* which was not as successful.

Two other Indiana natives participated in English's success in the 1940s. Clifton Webb appeared in a play, and Hoagy Carmichael staged a recital that was so popular that he performed there again the next day. Hoagy played the piano and sang a collection of the many hit songs he had created.

Comedies dominated the theater bookings at English's in the 1940s. One of the most popular was *Life with Father,* a portrait of a nineteenth-century family with a patient wife, a blustery tantrum-filled husband, and four active young sons. The three-act comedy by Howard Lindsay and Russell Crouse made six successful visits to the theater. Among other laughter producers were Joe E. Brown in *Harvey,* Boris Karloff in *Arsenic and Old Lace,* Edward Everett Horton in *Springtime for Henry,* and *The Philadelphia Story,* starring Katharine Hepburn, Van Heflin, and Joseph Cotten.

Dramas usually sold tickets at the theater, too. Alfred Lunt and Lynn Fontanne appeared in *There Shall Be No Night,* Todd Duncan in *Porgy and Bess,* and Ethel Barrymore in *The Corn Is Green.* The house was sold out for *Show Boat,* just a little over two months before its long life came to an end.

English's went dark after a Saturday evening performance of *Blossom Time,* one of the many Sigmund Romberg operettas that had been seen at the theater. The closing date was May 1, 1948. Apparently there was hope that this would only be temporary. The media were unusually quiet or were just not informed. It was late August before the *Indianapolis Star* reported that there was speculation the theater was doomed. This was all but confirmed when its manager, Vincent Burke, accepted a staff position at the Murat.

In October, the *Star* reported that the English Hotel would be razed but that a court ruling temporarily stopped a sale of the theater by the English Foundation to Equitable, which planned to lease the theater site to the J. C. Penney Company.

On December 26, it was revealed that the theater would be demolished. Late in February 1950, the lot was described as "just being a hole in the ground," to the sorrow of many. Eventually, the theater and the hotel would become the site for a J. C. Penney store.

The Murat stepped up with a heavier schedule than ever as Burke teamed up with Melvin Ross and formed Theater Productions, Inc. They would book Broadway productions into the Murat after it was renovated during the summer break. This provided the facility with a new stage, carpeting, drapes, and curtains. Seventy-five more seats were added, bringing the capacity to 2,000.

The series was launched with *Annie Get Your Gun;* Jean Parker in *Born Yesterday; Oklahoma,* now with Hoosier Wilton Clary as Curly; and Maurice Evans doing *Man and Superman.* These had to be scheduled around previous commitments to the Indianapolis Symphony Orchestra. The Murat lost some traveling productions because bookers wanted their shows to include Saturday, always a desirable ticket seller.

The Murat finished up the year with *Brigadoon,* Eddie Foy Jr. in *High Button Shoes,* Frank Fay in *Harvey,* Anthony Quinn in *A Streetcar Named Desire,* and Rex Harrison in *Anne of the Thousand Days.* By now, theatergoers had experienced some changes downtown and in their neighborhoods. The 1950s would confront them with many more.

187

Facing. Clifton Webb departed Indianapolis for the first time with his mother at the age of three. His English theater visit lasted one week in 1940, when he had the lead in Moss Hart and George S. Kaufman's comedy *The Man Who Came to Dinner.* He is shown here with actress Lupe Velez. Vincent Burke Collection.

The 1950s Bring Changes and New Competition

Facing. In the summer of 1953, the Indiana installed equipment that provided directional sound and tripled the size of the video on an enlarged screen. Bass Photo Company Collection, Indiana Historical Society.

Television came to town during the final months of the 1940s. WFBM-TV, Channel 6 (later WRTV) signed on with live coverage of the 500-Mile Race. Five months later, the area's second TV station arrived. WTTV, based in Bloomington, was seen in Indianapolis thanks to various-sized home antennae. Sixteen months after sign-on, Channel 6 was providing live network programming, and a year later, WTTV Channel 10 (which later became Channel 4) was granted a power increase and network service.

Viewers now were able to see movies in their homes. Granted, most of them at first were not Academy Award winners, but they were a novelty, as were news, sports, music, soap operas, and locally produced entertainment. Local TV personalities hosted movie presentations, and more and more films became available as more and more people purchased TV sets.

By 1954 the city had a third station, WISH-TV, Channel 8, and in 1957 it acquired a fourth, WLW-I, which later became WTHR, Channel 13. A remarkable moment occurred in January 1959 when Channel 13 equipment and personnel moved into the Indiana Theater for an evening to introduce and dedicate new studios. Video was shown on Indiana's screen and live entertainment was provided by cowboy star Gene Autry and local broadcast personalities headed by veteran talk show hostess Ruth Lyons. Her daily show was fed to 13 by WLW-TV in Cincinnati. Both stations were owned by Crosley, Inc.

The Indiana's owners decided early not to oppose this new form of entertainment. In February 1952, they ran a newspaper advertisement: "See history in the making . . . theater television in addition to a regular screen show." The TV attraction was a basketball game between Indiana University and the University of Illinois. It came direct from the IU Fieldhouse through the cooperation of IU and WTTV. It was noted that nearly 3,000 packed the theater. No one paid more than a dollar. A review in the *Indianapolis Star* was not all favorable, however. It stated that "faces and numerals of players were not distinct," and commercials had a similar problem.

Possibly because of the questionable visibility, college basketball on the theater's screen was attempted just one more time. It then turned to college football (three Notre Dame games). That eventually was abandoned, too. But video kept improving, and home screens kept getting larger. The theater then turned to boxing. Eight fights were scheduled. These involved such pugilists as Rocky Marciano and Ezzard Charles (matched up three times), Archie Moore, Sugar Ray Robinson, and Jersey Joe Walcott. In a sudden turnaround, the theater decided to

offer a live TV report of an opening night performance at the Metropolitan Opera House in New York City. Top price for this was $5. Audience response was modest, and theater television at the Indiana was terminated temporarily.

The new process was called CinemaScope. Its first feature was *Shane,* a western drama with Alan Ladd, Van Heflin, and Jean Arthur. It occupied the Indiana for two weeks. Six months later, *The Robe,* a big-screen interpretation of a novel centered on the aftermath of the Crucifixion, stayed an unprecedented seven weeks.

By 1954 the Circle, Keith's, and Loew's all had big-screen capability. The Lyric did not alter its facilities until the summer of 1956, when it added Todd-AO, another enhanced screen system. This enabled it to present the film version of *Oklahoma,* which stayed ten weeks. After that, advertisements claimed the theater was one of "ten in the world" to show *The Ten Commandments,* which stayed six months. That engagement was matched by *Around the World in Eighty Days,* which ran from early August to early February 1958. All this success continued because the lucky Lyric's next super film was *South Pacific.* It set another record, staying for more than eleven months.

This was surprising because the Lyric previously had been showing features that moved for additional weeks from the Indiana and Circle. Its films had rarely been first-run. Sometimes the theater had opened up its stage again for primarily country-western presentations. On came the *Grand Ole Opry Jamboree, Renfro Valley Barn Dance,* and such stars as Little Jimmy Dickens, Roy Acuff, Smiley Burnette, and Homer and Jethro. When Hank Snow and his Rainbow Ranch Boys paid a four-day visit, an extra added attraction came with them, a star of the future, Elvis Presley.

One week the Lyric looked back to its big band past and booked Tommy Dorsey, his trombone, his orchestra, and what it called a "giant stage revue." Three years later, it was a big rock-and-roll show onstage featuring the Chuck Berry Trio. The top price at the Dorsey show, which included a movie, was $1. Top price at the rock show, which didn't, was $2.75.

Changes also occurred at Keith's, the other member of the Indiana, Circle, and Lyric family under the Greater Indianapolis Entertainment operation. For the first six years of the 1950s, its primary job was the same as the Lyric's, showing holdover films from the Indiana and the Circle. One of the rare exceptions was a week when it claimed to offer a world premiere of *Sweethearts on Parade,* starring Bill Shirley, who grew up in Indianapolis. The Republic film booking was limited to one week.

After a six-week shutdown, it reopened its doors with *Guys and Dolls,* which had a stay of just under seven weeks. It was a new experience, similar to what was happening at the Lyric. Weeks later, the theater announced it had been selected

Keith's eventually installed CinemaScope and new sound equipment that guided it into a more independent operation in time
for the booking of *Carousel*. Courtesy *Indianapolis Star*.

for a state premiere of an upgraded big-screen version called CinemaScope 55.
The film was *Carousel*. This was followed by a series of big-screen features from
20th Century Fox and Paramount.

Suddenly when all seemed to be going so well, Keith's announced it was closing. This was at a time when a Keith's spokesman told the *Indianapolis Star* that
it was experiencing "one of the most successful seasons in its history." However, it
was further stated that at the moment there weren't enough major films to supply
suitable entertainment, and it would use the time to rebuild its facility. It concentrated on its interior. New additions included a garden entrance lobby, new seats,

curtains, draperies, and carpeting. The theater reopened in July 1957 with 800 invited guests and *The Prince and the Show Girl* starring Marilyn Monroe and Laurence Olivier.

Keith's finished out the 1950s with some of the top big-screen films of the time. Among them were *The Pajama Game, Sayonara, No Time for Sergeants, Anatomy of a Murder,* and *The Diary of Anne Frank.*

The popularity of the big band sound was fading rapidly by the early 1950s, but the Circle wrapped the era up with some of the best. Among those appearing were orchestras headed by Sammy Kaye, Frankie Carle, Eddy Duchin, Tommy Dorsey (featuring drummer Buddy Rich), Vaughn Monroe, Duke Ellington, and Ralph Flanagan, the latter with vocalist Patti Page. A few years later, there were one-day appearances by Stan Kenton and his "Festival of Modern Jazz," with vocalist June Christy. Orchestras headed by Fred Waring and Benny Goodman also were booked.

With the previous exceptions, the Circle primarily was a movie house in the 1950s. By 1953 it had the enlarged screen and the more sophisticated audio systems. In 1954 it showed Bing Crosby in *White Christmas,* for the first time in Vista Vision. It stayed five weeks. The movie menu included two Academy Award winners, *All about Eve* and *The Greatest Show on Earth,* the latter based on the development of the Ringling Brothers–Barnum and Bailey Circus. Some of its most popular films had comedy themes. Five featured Indianapolis-born Clifton Webb, six starred Donald O'Connor and his "talking" horse, and five others were about Ma and Pa Kettle, starring Hoosier Marjorie Main and Percy Kilbride.

Two other uses of the Circle stage had very little in common. The first was a one-day show titled *Top Record Stars of '56.* Its stars included Al Hibbler, Chuck Berry, and Illinois Jacquet with a "Big Rockin' Rhythm Band." The other presentation was a seven-day engagement of the seventeenth-century *Oberammergau,* a play that originated in the German city by the same name and dealt with Christ's last days on earth. It offered a large cast and twenty-five scenes.

Rare use of the stage continued at Loew's in the '50s. The first and last stage production of this decade was provided by the Metropolitan Opera Company. It presented *Die Fledermaus* in English. Apparently it was a success. The *Indianapolis Star* observed that some of those in attendance ate popcorn, which probably didn't happen often in New York City. There were two performances.

More typically at Loew's were some of the top movies of the time. Four of them won Academy Award honors. *The Bridge on the River Kwai* with Alec Guinness and *From Here to Eternity* with Frank Sinatra, Burt Lancaster, and Deborah Kerr stayed five weeks. Surprisingly, Gene Kelly in *An American in Paris* was gone after twenty-one days. Local audiences were even less responsive to a fourth Academy winner: Marlon Brando in *On the Waterfront,* which departed after one week.

The Circle delayed big-screen capability, serving its customers with first-run double features and a few months of swing band bookings onstage. Bass Photo Company Collection, Indiana Historical Society.

Loew's specialized in happy, upbeat musicals provided primarily by MGM. A few of them seen for the first time in Indianapolis were *On the Town, Singin' in the Rain, Hit the Deck, High Society,* and *Kiss Me Kate,* with music by Cole Porter. By 1953 the theater had joined the competition in providing big-screen viewing and 3D audio.

Although the city's largest theater (Indiana) was to lead the field in electronic advances that included live big-screen television, this did not guarantee a rosy future. No patrons were aware when on a Saturday evening an unwelcomed guest forced himself into a main floor office, armed with a pistol. Manager Al Hendricks, with a gun pressed against his back, handed over all the cash that he and his staff had been counting. The bandit departed with $4,500. In a front-page story the next day, the *Star* called the search that followed "one of the biggest downtown manhunts in recent years." The search was not successful, and it was not the kind of publicity a theater welcomed.

Five and a half years later, the Indiana announced it was closing as a cinema. This was startling, since it usually was chosen over the other Greater Indianapolis Amusement houses for first downtown showings of anticipated hits from 20th Century Fox, Universal-International, Warner Brothers, Paramount, and RKO Radio. Those studios provided the latest films by Bob Hope, Bing Crosby, Clifton Webb, and Dean Martin and Jerry Lewis.

The policy change at the big theater in 1958 was justified by a decision to use it as a convention center. Manager Maurice DeSwert was quoted in the *Indianapolis Star* as saying that "response for meetings and conventions has been much greater than we expected." He added, "It may show occasional films only if it isn't booked for other events."

The theater went dark for twenty days. Entertainment didn't really leave. A show of rock music appeared one day followed by a film of the Bolshoi Ballet, shown for two days. A week later, Benny Goodman and his orchestra played jazz for two and a half hours. This was followed by live plays. Eddie Bracken starred in *Tunnel of Love* for three days, as did Peter Ustinov in the comedy hit *Romanoff and Juliet*. By December, Leif Erickson had played FDR in *Sunrise at Campobello*. There were other appearances by the Dave Brubeck Quartet and an Indianapolis Symphony Orchestra Pops Concert. One week before Christmas, the Indiana was back in business with weekly bookings on the screen and onstage. There may have been some meetings during this time, but no conventions were mentioned.

Something else was happening that may have forced the Indiana to attempt a policy change: outdoor movies. By the early 1950s, there were eleven drive-ins, most of them in metropolitan Indianapolis. These outlets were popular with the younger crowd (it was not a costly date) and with young families who could let their children fall asleep in the backseat.

Neighborhood theaters were beginning a decline in the 1950s. Most but not all ran advertisements in the local daily newspapers at least once a week. On January 1, 1950, forty neighborhood movie outlets were listed. That number had dropped to fifteen by January 3, 1960, before shopping malls began providing multiple screen outlets in growing suburban areas.

When the decade began, the neighborhood theater business looked bright. Foreign films were becoming popular and frequently opened at a neighborhood house. They still were rarely seen in the downtown mainline theaters.

The Esquire, 2961 N. Illinois Street, was a leader not only in booking foreign films in Indianapolis but also in booking films that were considered unsuitable

The Arlington at East Tenth and North Arlington Avenue opened in October 1949, the first new standard neighborhood house built in ten years. In all probability, it was the last of its kind to be newly built in the Indianapolis area. Bass Photo Company Collection, Indiana Historical Society.

for young adults. An example of this was *The Moon Is Blue,* which used the words *virgin, mistress,* and *seduction,* linking them with humor. It was at the Esquire for thirty-one weeks. Downtown theaters were going through a morality period at the time, and Greater Indianapolis Amusement turned down *The Moon Is Blue* because it didn't have the motion picture industry's seal of approval. That opened the door for first-run films to venture out of the downtown area.

Although The French Line had been banned in St. Louis after it had been displayed there briefly, and despite condemnation by the Catholic Legion of Decency and the Protestant Motion Picture Council, it was the second time a Jane Russell film was not banned in Indianapolis. Attempts were made when her first film, The Outlaw, came to the Loew's in 1946. Star theater critic Corbin Patrick had called her "a hard and moody brunette who shows little promise as an actress." After a local group viewed The Outlaw for possible obscenity, former mayor Robert Tyndall was quoted as saying "he could see nothing obscene in it," and he added that he admired "a lot of nice mountain scenery."

Six months later, actress Jane Russell, known for what *The Filmgoer's Companion* called her "physical attributes," made local headlines. Her latest film, *The French Line*, also had failed to receive acceptance by the Association of Motion Picture Producers.

Local Parent Teacher Association officials, after viewing the film, called it "indecent" and asked Marion County Prosecutor Frank Fairchild to prevent its showing. It was scheduled to appear at three drive-ins along with the Ambassador, Ritz, and Tuxedo theaters. Fairchild filed charges against four Marion County theater owners and the film's distributor for exhibiting obscene pictures.

This came after Marion County Superior Court Judge John Niblack ruled that the prosecutor at least temporarily could not interfere with the showing of the film or seize copies of it. The State Supreme Court agreed. The anti-Russell battle ended when the PTA backed off and refused to help Fairchild's plan to run the film out of town. The organization's council decided its responsibilities did not include censorship.

Neighborhood theaters, some of them near the edge of downtown, continued to be more aggressive in booking foreign films. It was the Esquire where Indianapolis audiences first saw the Italian film *Bicycle Thieves*. *Filmgoer's Companion* called it a film that was "hailed throughout the world as the fount of Italian post-war realism." Alec Guinness films were first seen at the Esquire and the Ritz. There also were times when the Esquire moved into another category of film entertainment.

Raw sex films were appearing at the Ambassador and the Regent, both downtown on Illinois Street. Sometimes they may have overstated their subject. One week the Regent billed *Isle of Love*, starring Ingrid Bergman, for "adults only." Then there was the week the same theater offered *A Fig Leaf for Eve* and *Sinful Daughters* for 50¢ a ticket.

Onstage, strippers still were seen daily at the Fox. By 1953, it was alone in this category after the Mutual closed. Some of these performers were so successful that they were rebooked. Evelyn West and her "$50,000 Treasure Chest" visited the Fox seven times during the '50s. However, the champion was Rose LaRose, "undisputed queen of Burlesk." She made twenty-one visits. The runner-up was Irma the Body, "six feet of sophisticated dynamite," who made eleven appearances.

During this same era, the Walker Theater offered split-week double features. Seldom did it use its stage. An annual exception was a Christmas show, using primarily local talent, with proceeds going to needy families. There were other theaters in its neighborhood, but it was the most stable, with advertisements promoting its offerings in the *Recorder*.

Civil rights began to change the weekly newspaper's entertainment page. Downtown theaters began running ads, and the paper began writing stories about downtown shows. Both the Indiana and the Murat were booking highly popular African American musicians. Previously they were seen downtown by whites only, with the exception of Tomlinson Hall and Indiana Avenue nightclubs.

During the '50s the Murat and Indiana ran ads for forty-five stage shows that featured such musical icons as Duke Ellington, King Cole, Bobby Hackett, Dave Brubeck, Ella Fitzgerald, Stan Kenton, Louis Jordan, and Louis Armstrong. It didn't always go smoothly. Suits were filed against the operators of the Indiana Roof, who were charged with violating an Indiana Civil Rights statute in June 1955. Nine people who had purchased tickets were not admitted to a dance that featured Armstrong and his orchestra. A settlement followed, and by early 1959 the Indiana Roof was running advertisements in the *Recorder*.

Although not as numerous as the Indiana and Murat, other downtown ads in the *Recorder* were placed by the Lyric, Circle, Keith's, Loew's, and Fox.

The city's theater story had passed its hundredth year in September 1958. It had had its ups and downs, but the ups won, providing young and old with entertainment ranging from nonsense to serious matters that may have made us all just a little better.

Four of the downtown theaters that were still here in the fall of 1958 played major roles in what happened during the first 100 years. They are closing in on another fifty years as this is written. But first, a look at what happened to some of the others. The Fox fought closing vigorously. Its stage policy ended in 1961 when it turned to films, calling itself "Home of Unusual Art Film." Early in 1970 it attempted to return to onstage burlesk (its spelling). It soon was back with "adult films," with titles that the *Star* and *News* refused to reveal in advertisements. In the summer of 1975, there was talk that it might become a dinner theater. That didn't happen, and the Fox story was over by December 1975.

Three other theaters went more quietly. All were running films at the time. Keith's closed in July 1964. Lyric fans attempted to stop the inevitable, which occurred in April 1969. Loew's ended its story in April 1970 with an X-rated film that was not identified in newspaper ads.

19

A Brief Look at What Happened Next

Four Indy theaters have continued to do what they were built to do: entertain. The Murat lost the Symphony Orchestra in 1963 to the newly constructed Clowes Hall on the campus of Butler University. But with Cecil Byrne as its leader, the Murat continued to book musical shows and concert entertainers. It also became the home of the Indianapolis Opera Company before it shifted to Clowes.

Sunshine Productions managed the Murat after Byrne's retirement, and despite resistance regarding costs that involved the city, a multimillion dollar renovation took place in 1996. Two years later, the renamed Murat Centre and Clowes entered into an agreement to share a Broadway series each season.

The Circle went dark in 1981. It underwent a $6 million restoration and reopened in 1984 as the home of the Indianapolis Symphony Orchestra. The Indiana shut down its movie schedule in 1976, resurfaced for a while with pops concerts, then went dark a few months later. It dodged destruction when the Indiana Repertory Theater launched a $4 million fund drive to revise its interior. It became home for IRT in October 1980 with two auditoriums, one with 650 seats and the other with 250.

The fourth survivor, the Walker Theater, functioned for over twenty-seven years as the lead movie and film house for African Americans. The need for it lessened with integration, and in 1965 it closed. The Indiana General Assembly finally ensured equal accommodations for all theatergoers with the passage of civil rights legislation in 1963, one year before similar action was taken by Congress. Ironically, integration of theater audiences was legalized in Indiana in 1885 in a civil rights law. In a December 1987 article for the *Indiana Magazine of History,* Emma Lou Thornbrough noted that the law was "so widely ignored that most citizens were probably unaware of its existence."

In 1983, the Walker Theater reopened. Lilly donated $300,000, and the Madame Walker Urban Life Center purchased and renovated the building at a cost of $2 million. Its stage has been more active ever since.

The Indianapolis Symphony Orchestra was a major participant when what would become Starlight Musicals offered concerts and operettas at the State Fairgrounds, Garfield Park, and the Butler Bowl. Starlight found permanence when a stage and theater seats were established at Butler Bowl. It became known as the Theatron, with many local citizens active in keeping it financially stable.

Starlight opened its new outdoor theater in 1955 and eventually offered many popular musicals with prominently known actors playing lead roles. Weather problems forced its owners and leaders to establish a roof overhead. Many years of success finally began to fade, and the shows ended in 1993. Meanwhile, the Indianapolis Symphony Summer concerts (launched in 1982) at Conner Prairie proved extremely popular.

Another summer attraction came to Indianapolis in the 1950s, and at first it struggled to find a suitable location and a name. This professional stock company, which also mixed local talent with nationally known performers, became known as the Avondale Playhouse. Its first season in its home at the newly established Meadows Shopping Center opened in 1958 and offered at least ten plays a season through 1966.

The city was fortunate to have two devoted and qualified theater critics during most of the first century of stage and screen entertainment, Walter Whitworth and Corbin Patrick.

The theater era continues, but in different ways. Dinner theater came to the city in 1973 with the opening of Beef and Boards at 9301 N. Michigan Road. It is still op-

Walter Whitworth was drama and musical critic for more than sixty years at the *Indianapolis News* (1921–1965). He was still working when he died at age 69. Courtesy *Indianapolis Star.*

Corbin Patrick had been art critic for the *Indianapolis Star* for sixty-one years when he retired in 1988 at 82. He traveled to New York every year to review new shows on Broadway, many of which ended up at English's and/or the Murat. He was a key figure in bringing a symphony orchestra to Indianapolis. In 1950 he estimated he'd seen 5,000 movies and still enjoyed "a good one." Courtesy *Indianapolis Star.*

My grandson Michael Reidy thoroughly enjoyed Laurel and Hardy's *Sons of the Desert*, sixty years after I was first introduced to the movie by my grandmother. Lifetouch National School Studios.

erating year-round at this writing. Clowes Hall with 2,200 seats was constructed at a cost of $3.5 million. Named after the late Lilly executive George H. A. Clowes, it opened in 1963 and continues to offer a wide variety of artistic entertainment by professionals and students.

Downtown, the former American Cabaret Theatre relocated and changed its name to the Cabaret. It returned to its cabaret roots with more intimate surroundings, headed by ACT veteran performer Shannon Forsell. Its new home is the Columbia Club.

The city is not without what some might call "off-Broadway" productions. The Phoenix presents its productions at a former church at 749 N. Park Avenue. Founded in 1983, it moved to its current location in 1988. This was the same year that Theatre on the Square was created at Fountain Square by Ron Spencer. It moved to 677 Massachusetts Avenue in 1993.

Longevity honors go to another Indianapolis theater that focused on local talent. It was created in 1914 as the Little Theater, and by 1929 it was the Civic Theater. It has a remarkable history that has included a who's who in Indianapolis on- and offstage.

Neighborhood theaters were replaced by numerous movie screens in shopping centers near and far from downtown Indianapolis. However, the Circle Centre still provides movie screens downtown.

A few years ago, a grandson of mine reached the age of eight, my age when my grandmother and I visited Loew's Palace and saw Laurel and Hardy on the screen in *Sons of the Desert*. Suddenly there it was once again, this time on videotape at a store that was selling movies. I just couldn't resist. I purchased it and showed it to my grandson, wondering if he would respond as I did all those years ago. To my amazement, Michael was overcome with laughter. For months he wanted to see it again and again. He appreciated it every bit as much as I did, if not more.

204

Michael's reaction proved to me that not everything changes, even when change seems to be going on all around us. Maybe that's what Ted Lewis meant when he delivered those special words of his from the Loew's stage: "Is everybody happy?" Grandmother and I were. Ted wasn't there for Michael. But yes, he was happy, too.

BIBLIOGRAPHY

Balio, Tino, ed. *The American Film Industry*. Madison: University of Wisconsin Press, 1976.

Blum, Daniel. *A Pictorial History of the American Theatre, 1860–1976*. 4th ed. Revised by John Willis. New York: Crown, 1977.

Bodenhamer, David, and Robert Barrows. *The Encyclopedia of Indianapolis*. Bloomington: Indiana University Press, 1994.

Bordman, Gerald Martin. *The Oxford Companion to American Theatre*. 2nd ed. New York: Oxford University Press, 1992

Bowers, Q. David. *Nickelodeon Theatres and Their Music*. Vestal, N.Y.: Vestal Press, 1986.

Brownlow, Kevin. *The Parade's Gone By*. New York: Knopf, 1968.

Davis, Charlie. *That Band from Indiana*. Oswego, N.Y.: Mathom, 1982.

Draegert, Eva. "Cultural History of Indianapolis: The Theater, 1880–1890." *Indiana Magazine of History,* March 1956.

Dunn, Jacob Piatt. *Greater Indianapolis*. Vol. 1. Chicago: Lewis, 1910.

Gladson, Gene. *Indianapolis Theaters from A to Z*. Indianapolis: Gladson Publications, 1976.

Gomery, Douglas. *Shared Pleasures: A History of Movie Presentation in the United States*. Madison: University of Wisconsin Press, 1992.

Gray, Ralph, ed. *Gentlemen from Indiana: National Party Candidates, 1836–1940*. Indianapolis: Indiana Historical Bureau, 1977.

Halliwell, Leslie. *The Filmgoer's Companion.* 6th ed. New York: Hill and Wang, 1977.

Hetherington, James R. *Indianapolis Union Station.* Carmel: Guild Press of Indiana, 2000.

Holloway, W. R. *Indianapolis: A Historical and Statistical Sketch of the Railroad City, a Chronicle of Its Social, Municipal, Commercial, and Manufacturing Progress, with Full Statistical Tables.* Indianapolis: Indianapolis Journal Press, 1870.

Leary, Edward A. *Indianapolis: The Story of a City.* Indianapolis: Bobbs-Merrill, 1971.

Muncie, Larry. *Irvington Stories.* Indianapolis: Irvington Historical Society, 1992.

Sanford, Herb. *Tommy and Jimmy: The Dorsey Years.* New Rochelle, N.Y.: Arlington House, 1972.

Schiedt, Duncan. *The Jazz State of Indiana.* Pittsboro, Ind.: Schiedt, 1977.

Shumaker, Arthur W. *A History of Indiana Literature.* Indianapolis: Indiana Historical Society, 1962.

Snyder, Robert W. *The Voice of the City: Vaudeville and Popular Culture in New York.* New York: Oxford University Press, 1989.

Stone, Fred. *Rolling Stone.* New York: Whittlesey House, McGraw-Hill, 1945.

Sulgrove, Berry Robinson. *History of Indianapolis and Marion County, Indiana.* Philadelphia: L. H. Everts, 1884.

Sullivan, William George. *English's Opera House.* Indianapolis: Indiana Historical Society, 1960.

Thornbrough, Emma Lou. "Breaking Racial Barriers to Public Accommodations in Indiana, 1935 to 1963." *Indiana Magazine of History,* December 1987, 305–306.

HOWARD CALDWELL is a retired Indianapolis TV newscaster.
He has written *Tony Hinkle: Coach for All Seasons* (1991), the
introduction to *Indianapolis* (1990), and an overview essay for
The Encyclopedia of Indianapolis (1994), all published by
Indiana University Press.

THE END

9780253354600

www.ingramcontent.com/pod-product-compliance
Lightning Source LLC
Chambersburg PA
CBHW050403110426
42812CB00006BA/1788